I0120889

INDIANS AND OTHER MISNOMERS OF THE UPPER GREAT LAKES

The True Indigenous Origins of Geographic Place Names

Phil Bellfy

Ziibi Press

Sault Ste Marie, MI

Indians and Other Misnomers of the Upper Great Lakes: The True Indigenous Origins of Geographic Place Names.
Copyright © 2023 by Phil Bellfy. All Rights Reserved.

This book contains images and materials protected under International and Federal US Copyright Laws and Treaties. Any unauthorized reprint or use of this material is prohibited. No part of this book may be reproduced or transmitted in any form by any means, electronic or mechanical, including photocopying, recording, or by any information storage and retrieval system without the express written permission from the author.

Cover photo copyright by Phil Bellfy.

ISBN 978-1-61599-742-8 paperback
ISBN 978-1-61599-743-5 hardcover
ISBN 978-1-61599-744-2 eBook

Ziibi Press is an imprint of
Modern History Press
5145 Pontiac Trail
Ann Arbor, MI
More information at https://ziibipress.com/
info@ModernHistoryPress.com
www.ModernHistoryPress.com

Tollfree 888-761-6268
FAX 734-663-6861

Distributed by Ingram (USA/CAN/AU), Bertram's Books (EU/UK)

Contents

Introduction

The United States of America contains 50 states, and 27 state names are rooted in American Indian languages. The modern nation of Canada consists of ten provinces and three territories: four of the provinces and two of the territories are names with indigenous origins, and, of course, Canada itself is derived from an indigenous source. In this volume, only Pennsylvania is from a non-native source.

So, *What's in a Name?* California and Florida (and others) reflect their Spanish history; here in the Great Lakes, that history is indigenous. If you have an understanding of the name of a place, its history may reveal itself.

And that history will, most likely, enrich your own life and your place in it.

This book's subtitle claims that the book contains the "true" indigenous meaning of Great Lakes' place names, but the reader should consider this—many of the place names were first recorded by Europeans during a time when Indigenous linguistics, and even spelling conventions, were in their infancy (at best). Consider that the Michigan village of Topinabee is named after a Potawatomie chief, whose name was spelled 12 different ways in 11 treaties, and, not one of those treaties spelled it the way the current village name is spelled!

And, as should be obvious, various spellings lead to various pronunciations, and, in turn, those various pronunciations may very well refer to indigenous words with different meanings. Indigenous languages of this hemisphere were not written languages; ours were and are oral traditions.

So, the reader will undoubtedly find entries that appear to be duplicates or entries of the same word with different meanings. That is because the author relies on different print sources and merely repeats what those sources contain. At the same time, the author made inquiries in every Indigenous community covered in this volume. Of course, many did not respond, but every Indigenous response is included. Again, these responses may not be the same as those in books cited in the References section of this volume.

Furthermore, in today's internet world, you can find any number of sites that purport to give you the translation of Native-based place names. I have included some of these, but not if they differ appreciably from the References sources, believing that the older the source, the more authentic the meaning—the *True Indigenous Origins* claimed in this book's subtitle.

I need to add a little about the US Royce maps in this book, and the list of land cession treaties. Just as it is vital to understand a place through an examination of its name, you cannot come to a true understanding of a place without a thorough understanding of the treaties through which those territories became part of the modern government states of which they are now an integral part.

As you can see in the "US Treaties" section of this book, the very first treaty signed by the US and Indigenous people was for the land cession of western Pennsylvania. Obviously, the eastern part of the state and, indeed, the entire colonial part of what is now the United States, had been taken over by the US before the treaty-making period; in this volume, starting in 1784 and ending in 1889.

In Canada, the first Ontario cession was signed in 1783; the last in 1930. Note that the Canadian list in this volume is not in chronological order, instead following the alphabetic order of the cessions as given by the Ontario government, creators of this volume's map.

It should also be noted that both in the US and in Canada, many land cession treaties are subject to ongoing interpretation, and, in many cases, litigation. In most of British Columbia, for example, land cession treaties are still being negotiated. The first modern British Columbia treaty, the Nisga'a Treaty, came into effect in 2000, and only three have been added since then (in 2009, 2011 and 2016).

Compared to Latin, considered to be a "dead" language, indigenous treaties (with both US and Canada) are very much living documents, and the names of places in both countries are alive, as well, subject to a more accurate naming and meaning. Miigwetch (thank you) for your interest in this subject and in this book. I hope you enjoy reading it as much as I did creating it!

P.C.B.

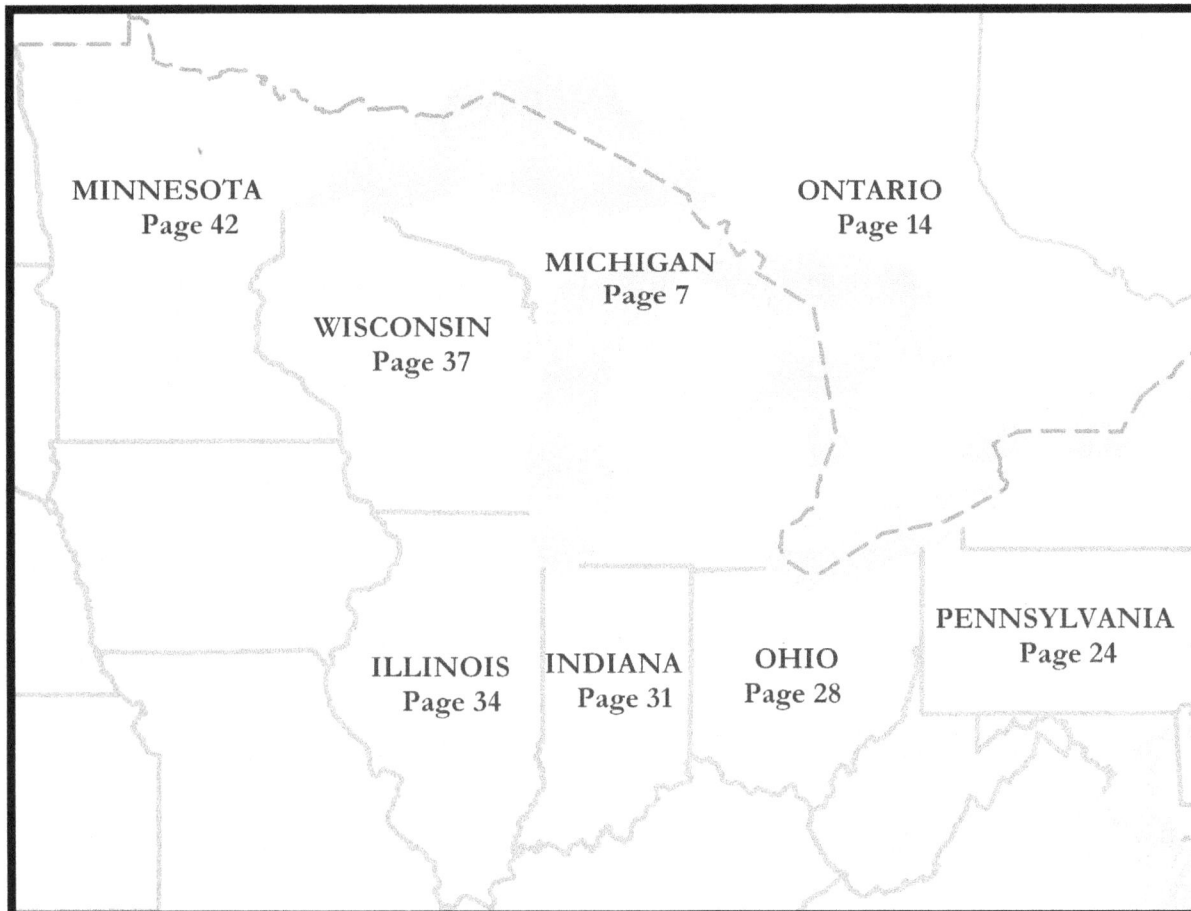

Geographic Scope of this Volume and Index to State and Province Place Names.

State and Provincial Maps

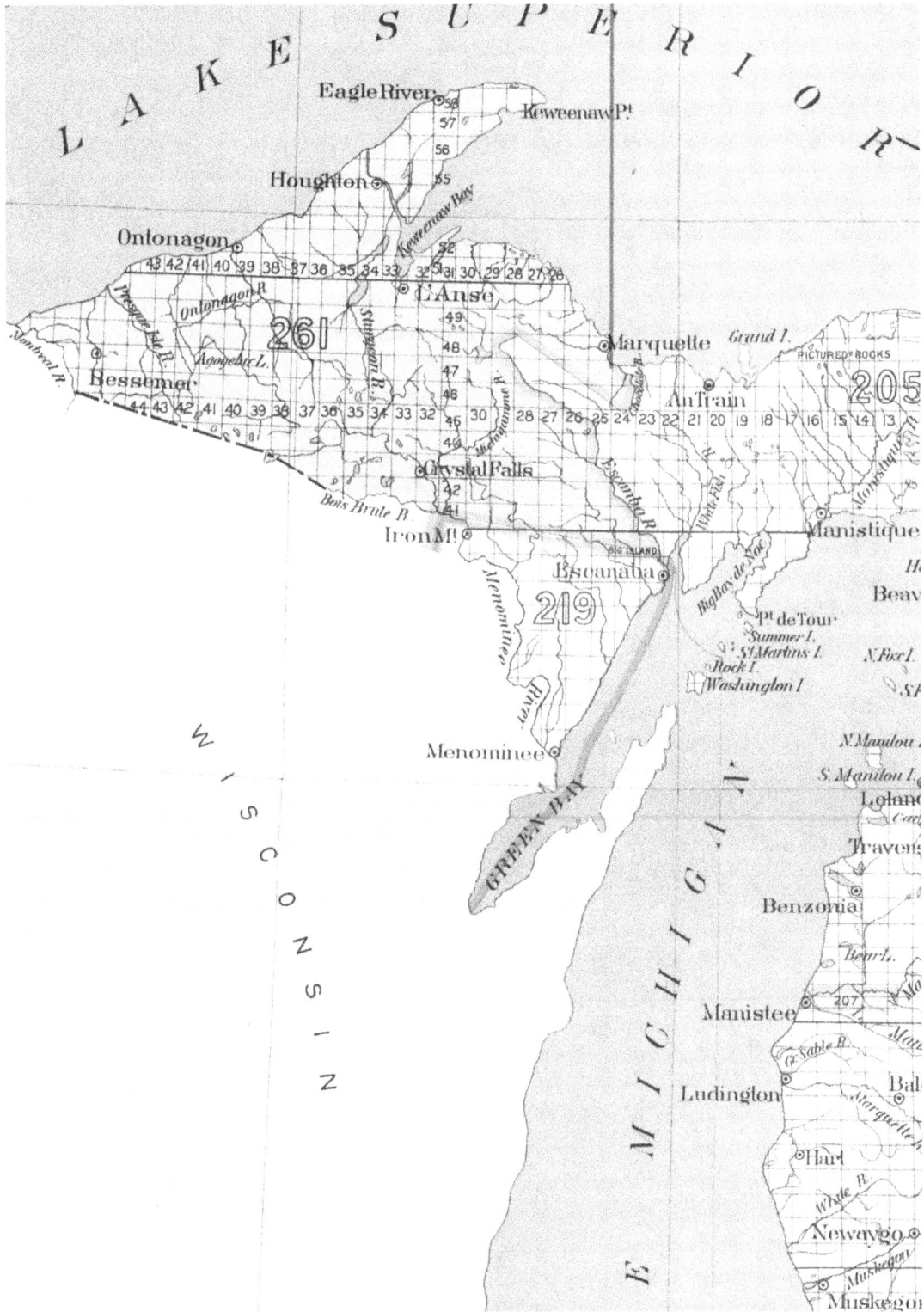

Royce Map of Michigan – West

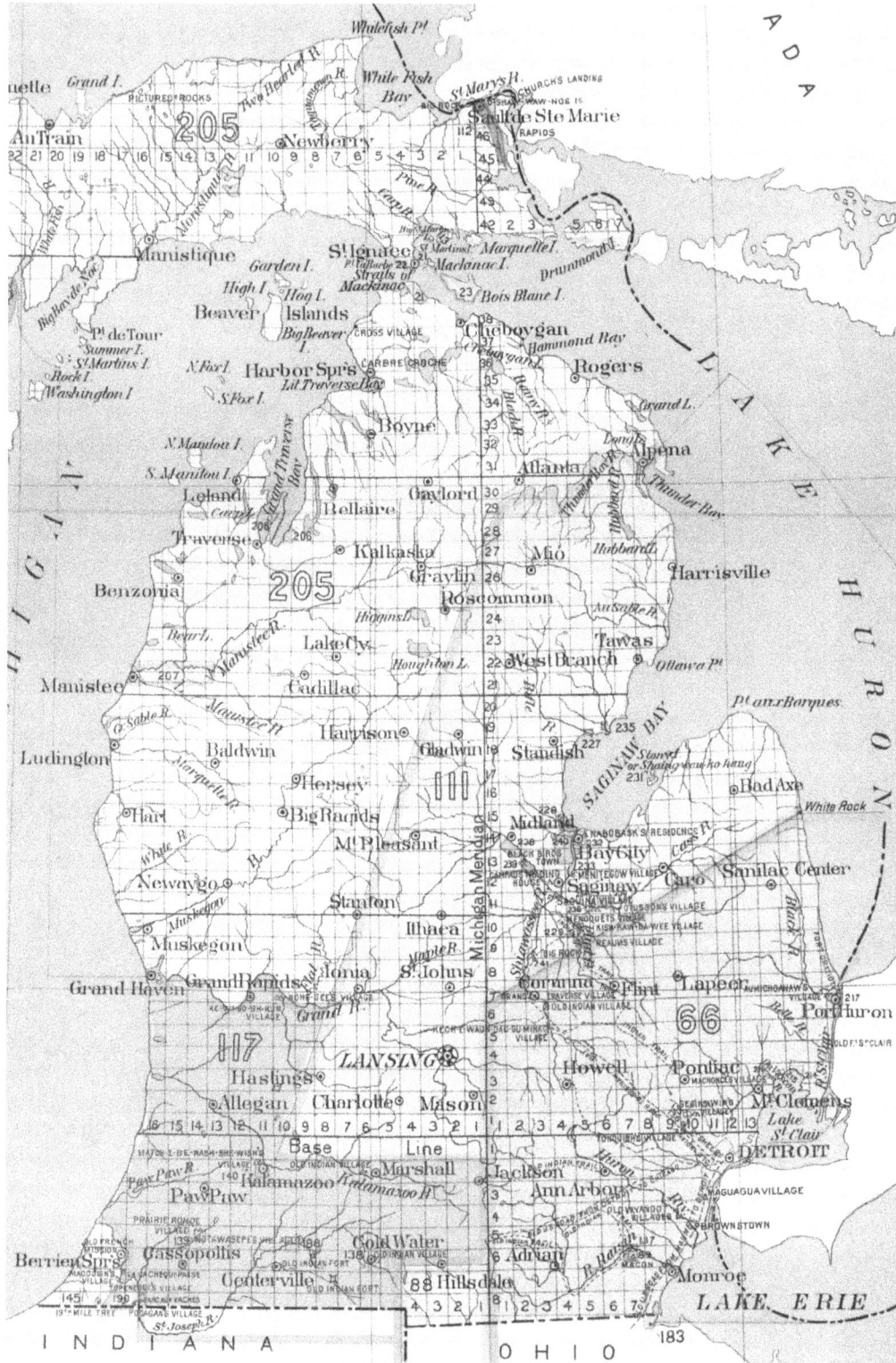

Royce Map of Michigan – East

Michigan Place Names

Michigan - most often translated as Big Lake; as in Michi (big) and Gammi (lake); or Mishi-gummeeng: Great Body of Water; other translations found were Majigan: Clearing, Majiigan: Large Clearing, and Mishi-maikin: Swimming Turtle. Used as a place name throughout the Midwest.

Notations used: p.n. = place name; t.s. = treaty signer; and ntg = no translation given.

Ahmeek: Beaver

Alcona: County given "Indian-sounding" name by Indian Agent Henry Rowe Schoolcraft

Allegan: County given "Indian-sounding" name by Indian Agent Henry Rowe Schoolcraft

Alpena: County given "Indian-sounding" name by Indian Agent Henry Rowe Schoolcraft, possibly meant to refer to the Partridge

Arenac: County given "Indian-sounding" name by Indian Agent Henry Rowe Schoolcraft

Bawating: River Beaten to a Spray, or Gathering Place of the People; orig. name for Sault Ste. Marie

Bay Mills Indian Community: aka Ginozhaekaunning: Pike Place. Michigan reservation.

Burt Lake Band of Ottawa and Chippewa Indians: State-recognized Tribe

Cheboygan: Pipe, or Funnel; or from Shabwawagoning: Rumbling Waters, or Waters Disappearing Underground

Chesaning: At the Big Rock

Chippewa, tribal name with various meanings; those found in reference to place names; Gathering Up Voice, Voice Gathered Up, or Puckered Voice see Ojibway for a complete discussion

Cohoctah: Many Trees in the Water

Detroit; orig. Wawiyatanong: Where the River Turns, or Crooked Way; Yondotiga: Great Village; or Karontaen: Coast of the Straits

Dowagiac: Subsistence Area, or Fishing Waters

Escanaba: Flat Rock. Or Land of the Red Buck

Genesee: Beautiful Valley

Gogebic: Green Lake, High Lake, On the Rock, or Trembling Ground

Grand River Band of Ottawa Indians: State-recognized Tribe

Grand Sable Dunes; orig. Nigowidjiw: Sand Mountain

Grand Traverse Band of Ottawa and Chippewa Indians: Reservation

Gun Lake: Match-e-be-nash-she-wish Band of Pottawatomi Indians: Bad Bird; (aka Gun Lake Tribe); Reservation

Hannahville Potawatomi Indian Community: Reservation

Hiawatha: River Maker

Iosco: County given "Indian-sounding" name by Indian Agent Henry Rowe Schoolcraft, possibly meant to refer to Shining Water, or Water of Light

Ishpeming: High Place

Juniata (Twp): Standing Rock

Kalamazoo, of Native origin, with several possible translations: It Smokes, Smoke, or Otter's Water; or from Kekekalakalamazoo: Where the Water Boils (or Smokes) in the Pot; or from Negikanamazo: Otter Tail, or Beautiful Water, Boiling Water, or Stones Like Otters; or from Kikalamozo: He Is Inconvienced By Smoke In His Lodge

Kalkaska: County given "Indian-sounding" name by Indian Agent Henry Rowe Schoolcraft, possibly meant to refer to Burned-Over Land

Kawkawlin: Pike Place

Kenockee: Long-legged

Keweenaw (Bay Indian Community): Cross A Point, or Portage; MI Reservation

Lac Vieux Desert (Band of Lake Superior Chippewa): Lake of the Old Garden Clearing; Reservation

Leelanau: County given "Indian-sounding" name by Indian Agent Henry Rowe Schoolcraft, possibly meant to refer to Delight of Life. There is no "L" sound in the Ojibway language.

Lenawee: County given "Indian-sounding" name by Indian Agent Henry Rowe Schoolcraft, possibly meant to refer to "Man." There is no "L" sound in the Ojibway language.

Les Chenaux; orig; Anaminang: In the Bowels (a reference to the channels' tortuous intricacy)

Little River Band of Ottawa Indians: MI Reservation

Little Traverse Bay Band of Odawa Indians: MI Reservation

Mackinac (also spelled, and pronounced, Mackinaw): from Michilimackinak; Large Turtle Island, or Place of the Great Turtle.

Mackinac Bands of Ottawa and Chippewa Indians: State-recognized Tribe

Manistee (and Manistique): Crooked River, Red River, Wind Sound, Lost River, Wood's Spirit, or Yellow Thunder

Manitou: Spirit

Match-e-be-nash-she-wish Band of Potawatomi Indians: Bad Bird; aka Gun Lake Tribe; Reservation

Meauwataka: Halfway (between two bodies of water)

Mecosta: Bear Cub

Menominee: Wild Rice People

Michigamme: Great Water

Missaukee: At the Big Outlet

Munising: Island in the Lake

Munuscong: Place of the Reeds

Muskegon: Swampy, or Marshy River; or from Maskegowok: Swamp People

Nahma: Sturgeon

Naubinway: Place of Echoes

Neahtawanta: Placid Waters

Neebish (Island): Leaf

Negaunee: He Walks Ahead (ie. the pioneer)

Nottawa: the Iroquois

Nottawaseppi Huron Band Potawatomi: Like Rattlesnakes; Reservation

Nunda: Where the Valley Meets the Hill

Ogemaw: Chief

Okemos: Secondary Chief, or Little Chief

Onaway: Awake

Onekama: Singing Water

Ontonagon: Place Where Game Was Shot By Luck

Osceola: Black Drink Hallower

Oscoda County: given "Indian-sounding" name by Indian Agent Henry Rowe Schoolcraft, possibly meant to refer to a Rocky Prairie

Oshtemo: Headwaters

Ossineke: Where the Pictographs Were

Otsego: Place of the Rock

Ottawa: To Trade

Painted Rocks: Mazinaubikaung

Peshawbestown: Odawa Reservation; named after local Chief

Petoskey: Where the Sun Shines Through the Clouds

Pinconning: Potato Place

Pokagon (Band of Potawatomi Indians): Something Used to Shield; Reservation

Ponshewaing: Peaceful Waters, or Winter Home

Pontiac: from Bonitiyak: Stops By Use of A Stick

Quinnesec: from Pekwenesseg: Where the River Forms A Spray

Saginaw (Chippewa Indian Tribe): Place of the Sac Tribe; Reservation

Sagola: "Welcome"

Sandusky: Water

Saranac: Sumac Cone River

Saugatuck: Tidal Outlet

Sault Ste. Marie (Tribe of Chippewa Indians): Reservation

Sault Ste. Marie: orig. Baweting: Place of the Rapids; Gathering Place of the People

Sebewa: Little Creek

Sebewaing: River Place

Shiawassee: Straight Ahead Water; or from Azhaowesse: River That Twists About

St. Clair (Lake) : orig. Wauwi-autinoong: Round Lake

Superior (Lake): orig. Kitchi-gummeng: Great Lake (of the Ojibway)

Swan Creek Black River Confederated Ojibwa Tribes of Michigan: State-recognized Tribe

Tahquamenon: Shallow Bed River, or Dark-colored Water

Tecumseh: Panther Crouching For Its Prey

Tekonsha: Resembling a Caribou

Tittabawassee: River Following the Line of the Lakeshore

Topinabee: He Who Sits Quietly; notable 19th c. Potawatomi chief who signed many treaties

Tuscola: County given "Indian-sounding" name by Indian Agent Henry Rowe Schoolcraft, possibly meant to refer to a Warrior Prairie, or Level Lands

Unadilla: Meeting Place

Waishkey: Buffalo (U.P. river)

Washtenaw: On the River, or Far Off

Waucedah: Talking Stream

Wequetonsing: At the Head of the Little Bay

Winona: First-Born Daughter

Wyandotte: Islanders, or Peninsula Dwellers

Wyoming: At the Big River Flat

Yuma: Sons of the River

Zeba: from Zibii: River

Indians Fishing in the Rapids, Sault Ste. Marie, Mich.
Courtesy Library of Congress.

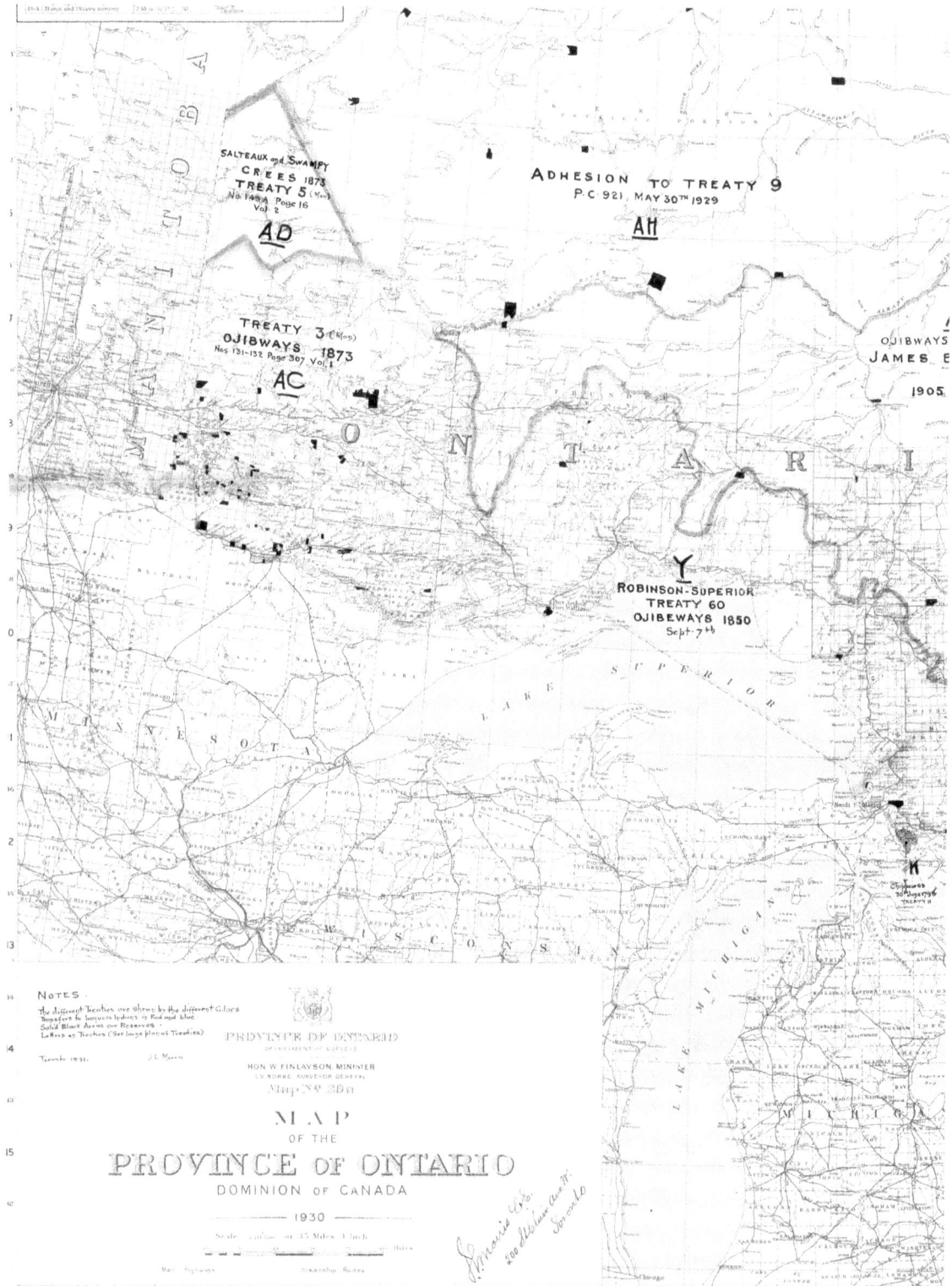

Map of Western Ontario

Map of Eastern Ontario

Ontario Place Names

ONTARIO; or from Kanadario: Sparkling Water; or from Onitariio: Beautiful Lake; or from Ontarack: Rocks Standing High in the Water; other possible meanings: Handsome Lake, or Large Lake; NY, OR, WI p.n. It should be noted that many Ontario First Nations have renamed their Reserves in their language, and the "translation" is not always given as an assertion of their original jurisdiction.

Notations used: p.n. = place name; t.s. = treaty signer; and ntg = no translation given.

Aamjiwnaang: Meeting Place By the Rapid Water, or At the Spawning Stream; First Nation

Abitibi: Half-way Water (in reference to trading posts in either direction)

Agawa Canyon: Bending Shore

Alderville: First Nation

Algonquin: Spearing Fish from the End of a Canoe, or Spearing Fish Place

Algonquins of Pikwàkanagàn: A Hilly Place; First Nation

Animbiigoo Zaagi'igan Anishinaabek (ntg): First Nation

Anishinaabeg of Naongashiing: Big Island: First Nation

Aroland: First Nation

Atikameksheng Anishnawbek: (ntg) formerly known as the Whitefish Lake First Nation

Atikokan: Caribou Bones

Attawapiskat: Rock Bottom; People of the Parting of the Rocks; First Nation

Baagwaashiing: Where the Water is Shallow; aka Pays Plat (French: Flat Land); First Nation

Batchewana: First Nation

Batchewana Bay: Welling Waters Place

Bearfoot Onondaga: First Nation

Beausoleil: First Nation

Beaverhouse: non-Status First Nation

Big Grassy: First Nation

Biinjitiwaabik Zaaging Anishinaabek (ntg): First Nation

Bkejwanong: Where the Waters Divide (Walpole Island); First Nation

Brantford: named after the prominent Mohawk chief, Joseph Brant

Brunswick House: First Nation

Caldwell: First Nation

Cat Lake: First Nation

Cataraqui: Where River and Lake Meet

Cayuga: Here They Take the Boats Out

Chapleau Cree: First Nation

Chippawa: People Without Moccasins

Chippewa of the Thames: First Nation

Chippewas of Georgina Island: First Nation

Chippewas of Kettle & Stony Point: First Nation

Chippewas of Mnjikaning: The Fish Fence at the Narrows; (aka Rama); First Nation

Chippewas of Nawash (formerly known as Cape Croker): First Nation

Chippewas of Saugeen: First Nation

Coaticook: River of Pines

Constance Lake; First Nation

Couchiching: Edge of a Whirlpool; or from Gojijing: Inlet; First Nation

Curve Lake: First Nation

Deer Lake: First Nation

Delaware: First Nation

Dokis: First Nation

Eabametoong First Nation: At the Reversing of the Waterplace

Eagle Lake: First Nation

Erie: Long-tailed, or Panther

Etobicoke: from Wahdobekaung; Forest of Alders, or Place Where Alders Grow

Flying Post: First Nation

Fort Albany: First Nation

Fort Severn: First Nation

Fort William: First Nation

Gananoque: Rocks in Deep Water, or Rocks Rising Out of River

Ginoogaming (formerly known as Long Lake 77): First Nation

Gogama: Fish Leap Over the Water

Grassy Narrows: aka Asubpeeschoseewagong (ntg); aka Iskapiciwan: Dried-up Stream; First Nation

Gull Bay: First Nation

Hiawatha: First Nation

Hornepayne: First Nation

Iroquois: Real Adders

Iskutewizaagegan: (ntg) (formerly known as Shoal Lake 39 First Nation)

Kakabeka Falls: River of Short Bends and Many Islands, or Always Plenty of Game

Kaministiquia: (River) With Islands

Kapuskasing: from Paskeshegay; Rushing Water, Shooting Water, or Bend in River

Kasabonika Lake: (ntg); First Nation

Kashechewan First Nation: Where the Water Flows Fast

Keewatin: North Wind Place

Keewaywin: Going Home, or Going Back; First Nation

Kenogami: Long Water

Kenora: a municipal name coined from KEewatin (see above), NOrman, and RAt Portage

Ketegaunseebee: Garden River First Nation

Kingfisher: First Nation

Komoka: Place Where the Dead Lie

Koocheching: (ntg); First Nation

Lac des Mille Lacs: First Nation

Lac La Croix: First Nation

Lac Seul: First Nation

Little Current: aka Waibejewung: Place Where the Waters Flow Back and Forth

Long Lake: First Nation

Madawaska: Grassy River Mouth; or People of the Shadows

Maganetewan: Long, Open Channel, or Swiftly Flowing River

Magnetawan: Swiftly Flowing Waters; First Nation

Manitoulin: Island of the Spirit; or a corruption of Manitowaning: At the Spirit's Cave (the root, Manitou, means Spirit)

Manitowaning: Great Spirit Cave

Marten Falls: First Nation

Matachewan: Meeting of the Currents; First Nation

Mattagami: Meeting of the Currents; First Nation

Mattawa: Where the Current Begins, River Flowing Into the Lake, or River Flowing Into Another Body of Water

McDowell Lake: First Nation

M'Chigeeng: Village Enclosed by Stepped Cliffs; First Nation

Michipicoten: Big Blufs, Bold Promontories Place, or Broken, Craggy Highlands Place; First Nation

Mimico: Wild Pigeon Place

Mindemoya, Lake: Old Woman Lake

Mishkeegogamang: (formerly known as Osnaburgh); First Nation

Missanabie Cree: Pictured Water: First Nation

Missinaibi: Pictures on the Water (reference to pictographs along banks)

Mississauga: River Having Many Outlets; First Nation

Mississaugas of Scugog Island: Swampy or Marshy Land; First Nation

Mississaugas of the Credit: First Nation

Mnjikaning First Nation: Near the Fishing Weirs

Mocreebec Indian Government: First Nation

Mohawks of Akwesasne: Land Where the Partridge Drums; First Nation

Mohawks of the Bay of Quinte: First Nation

Moose Cree: First Nation

Moose Deer Point: First Nation

Moosonee: At the Moose (River)

Munsee-Delaware Nation: First Nation

Muskoka: Red Earth; or from Mesqua Ukie: (Chief) Yellowhead

Muskrat Dam Lake: First Nation

Naicatchewenin: At the Place Where the Current is Obstructed; First Nation

Nakina: Land Covered with Moss

Namaygoosisagagun: Trout Lake (non-Status); First Nation

Nanticoke: Tide-water

Naotkamegwanning Anishinabe: Of the Whitefish Point; First Nation

Napanee: Flour

Nassagaweya: River with Two Outlets

Neebing: Summer

Neskantaga (ntg): First Nation

Netmizaaggamig Nishnaabeg (ntg): (formerly Pic Mobert); First Nation

Niagara: Bisected Bottom Lands, Neck of Land Between Lakes, Thunder of Waters, or Resounding with Great Noise; aka Kitchi-Gaugeedjiwunng: Great Falls

Nibinamik First Nation: Summer Beaver

Nigigoonsiminikaaning First Nation: Place Abundant with Little-Otter Berries

Niisaachewan Anishinaabe Nation: (ntg); First Nation

Nipigon: So Long that You Cannot See the End of It; or from Animibeegoong: Along the Water's Edge, or Continuous Water

Nipissing, Lake: At the Place of the Waters; or In a Little Water, or In the Leaves; or from Nipisisinan: Little Body of Water (ie. the smallest of the Great Lakes); First Nation

North Caribou Lake: First Nation

North Spirit Lake: First Nation

Northwest Angle No. 33: First Nation

Northwest Angle No. 37: First Nation

Ojibways of Garden River: First Nation

Ojibways of Onigaming: The Portage; First Nation

Ojibways of Sucker Creek: First Nation

Ojibways of the Pic River: First Nation

Onaping: from Onumananing: Red Paint, or Vermillion

Oneida Nation of the Thames: First Nation

Oneida: People of the Upright Stone

Opeongo: Sandy at the Narrows

Oshawa: To Go to the Other Side, Stream Crossing, or Carrying Place

Otonabee: River That Beats Like a Heart

Ottawa: Bartering Place, To Trade; Basil Johnston, an Ojibway speaker, says the word means To Sell, not To Trade; he also says that the Ottawa River is named from Odauwuhnshk, which means Bullrush River

Parry Island: orig. Waussaukissing: Brightly Reflecting

Peawanuck: Flintstone; new name for Winisk

Penetanguishene: Place of White Falling Sands, or Where the Sand Slides Down the Bank

Petawawa: Noise of Water Far Away is Heard

Pikangikum: Lake of Calm Waters; First Nation

Pikwakanagan First Nation: Hilly Place, or Hlly Country Covered in Evergreens

Poplar Hill: First Nation

Poplar Point: First Nation

Powassan: Big Bend

Rainy River: Ojiji Ziibi; First Nation

Red Rock Band: First Nation

Sabaskong: Passage Way

Sachigo Lake (ntg): First Nation

Sagamok Anishnawbek: Two Points Joining, or Many Rivers Joining; First Nation

Sand Point: First Nation

Sandy Lake: First Nation

Sarnia: orig. Aumidjiwunaung: Place Where the Waters Collect

Saugeen: Zaagiing; At the Mouth of the River; First Nation

Sault Ste. Marie; orig. Baweting: Gathering Place of the People, Place of the Rapids, or River Beaten to a Spray

Scugog: Muddy Bottom, Submerged Land, or Waves Leap Over a Canoe

Seine River: First Nation

Serpent River: First Nation

Shawanaga: Long Bay or Strait, or South Portage; First Nation

Sheboygan: Great Noise

Sheguiandah: Bay of Gray Slate; First Nation

Sheshegwaning: (ntg); First Nation

Shingwauk: Place of Pines

Shoal Lake: First Nation

Shuniah: Money, or Silver

Six Nations of the Grand River: First Nation

Slate Falls: First Nation

Spadina: from Ishapadenah: Hill (Toronto Street name)

St. Clair (Lake): orig. Wauwi-autinoong: Round Lake

Stanjikoming (a true misnomer with no meaning in any Indigenous language): changing name to Mitaanjigamiing: Where Shallow Water Runs into Deep Water; First Nation

Superior (Lake): orig. Kitch-gummeng: Great Lake (of the Ojibway)

Taykwa Tagamou: (ntg) (formerly known as New Post); First Nation

Tecumseh: Panther Crouching for its Prey

Temagami: Deep Water by the Shore; First Nation

Temiscaming: Deep Dry Water Place (dry in summer)

Thessalon: from Neyashewun: Point of Land; First Nation

Thomas Bay (on Manitoulin Island): aka Wanoshkang Bay: You Must Go Around

Thunder Bay: from the Native, Animikie-Wekwed; orig. Gamanautigawaeyauk: Land of Many River Islands

Timagami: Deep Water

Timiskaming: Deep Water, or In the Deep Water

Toronto: Fallen Trees in the Water, or Meeting Place; or from Deondo: Trees Growing Out of the Water; or from Kanitareonto: Bay in the Lake, or Opening; or from Thorontohen: Timbers on the Water

Wabaseemoong First Nation: Whitedog

Wabigoon: Marigold, or White Feather; First Nation

Wahgoshig: Little Fox; First Nation

Wahnapitae: Place Where Water is Shaped Like a Tooth; First Nation

Wahta Mohawks: Sugar Maple; First Nation

Wapekeka: (ntg) (formerly known as Angling Lake First Nation); First Nation

Wasauksing First Nation: Place that Shines Brightly in the Reflection of the Sacred Light

Wasauksing: (formerly Parry Island First Nation); First Nation

Washagamis Bay: (also Obashkaandagaang) (ntg); First Nation

Wauzhushk First Nation: Portage to the Country of the Muskrats

Wawa: Cry of the Wild Goose, or simply Wild Goose

Wawakapewin First Nation: Long Dog Lake

Wawanosh: Beautiful Sailor

Webequie First Nation: Shaking Head

Weenusk First Nation: Groundhog

Whitesand: First Nation

Whitewater Lake: First Nation

Wikwemikong: Bay of Beavers; Unceded Indian Territory; First Nation

Winisk: now called Peawanuck: Flintstone

Wunnumin First Nation: Vermillion Lake

Wyoming: At the Big River Flat

Zhiibaahaasing: (ntg) (formerly Cockburn Island 19A); First Nation

Battle of the Thames River, Ontario, depicting the death of Tecumseh, October 5, 1813.
Image courtesy of Library of Congress.

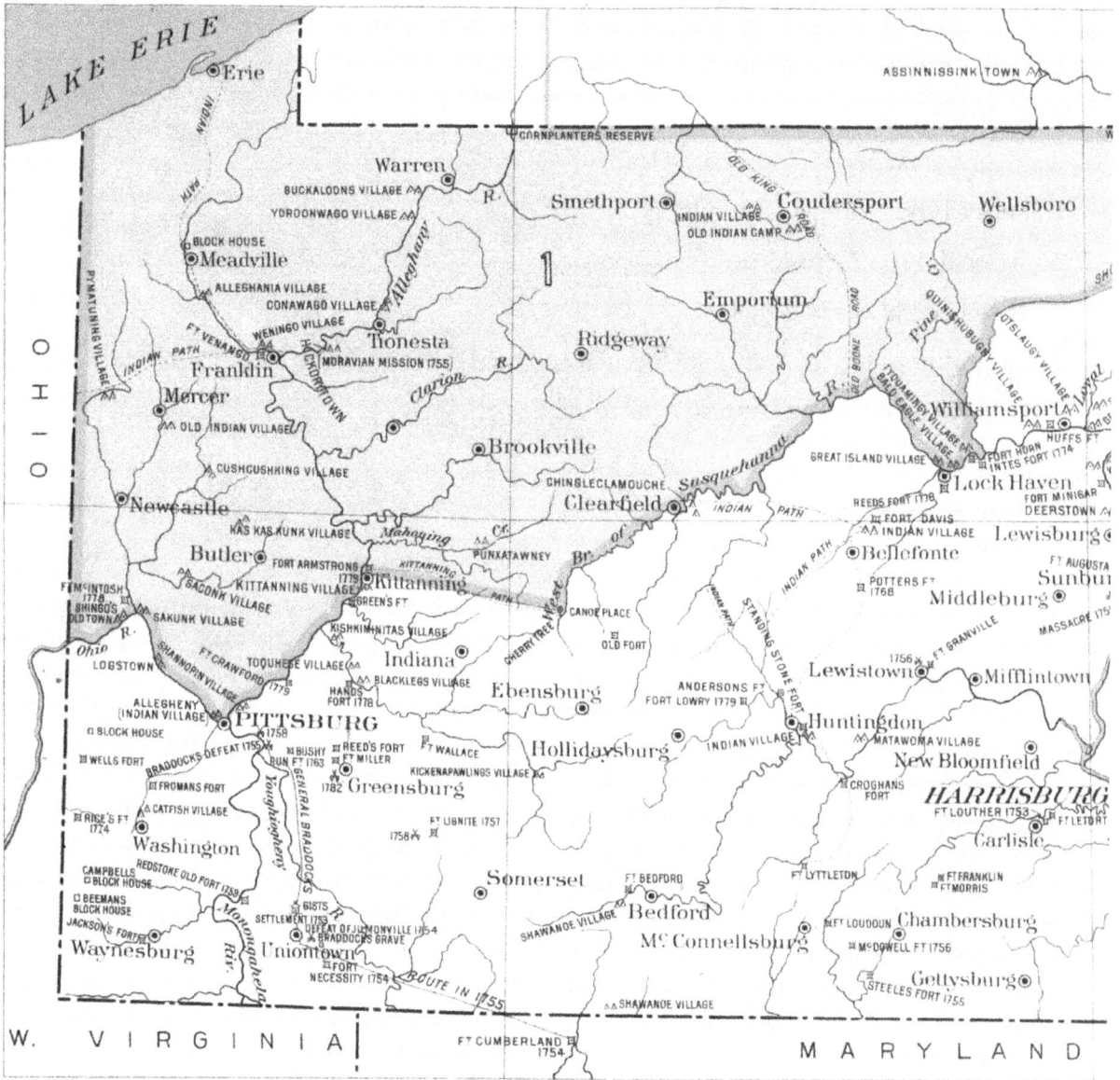

Royce Map of Pennsylvania - West

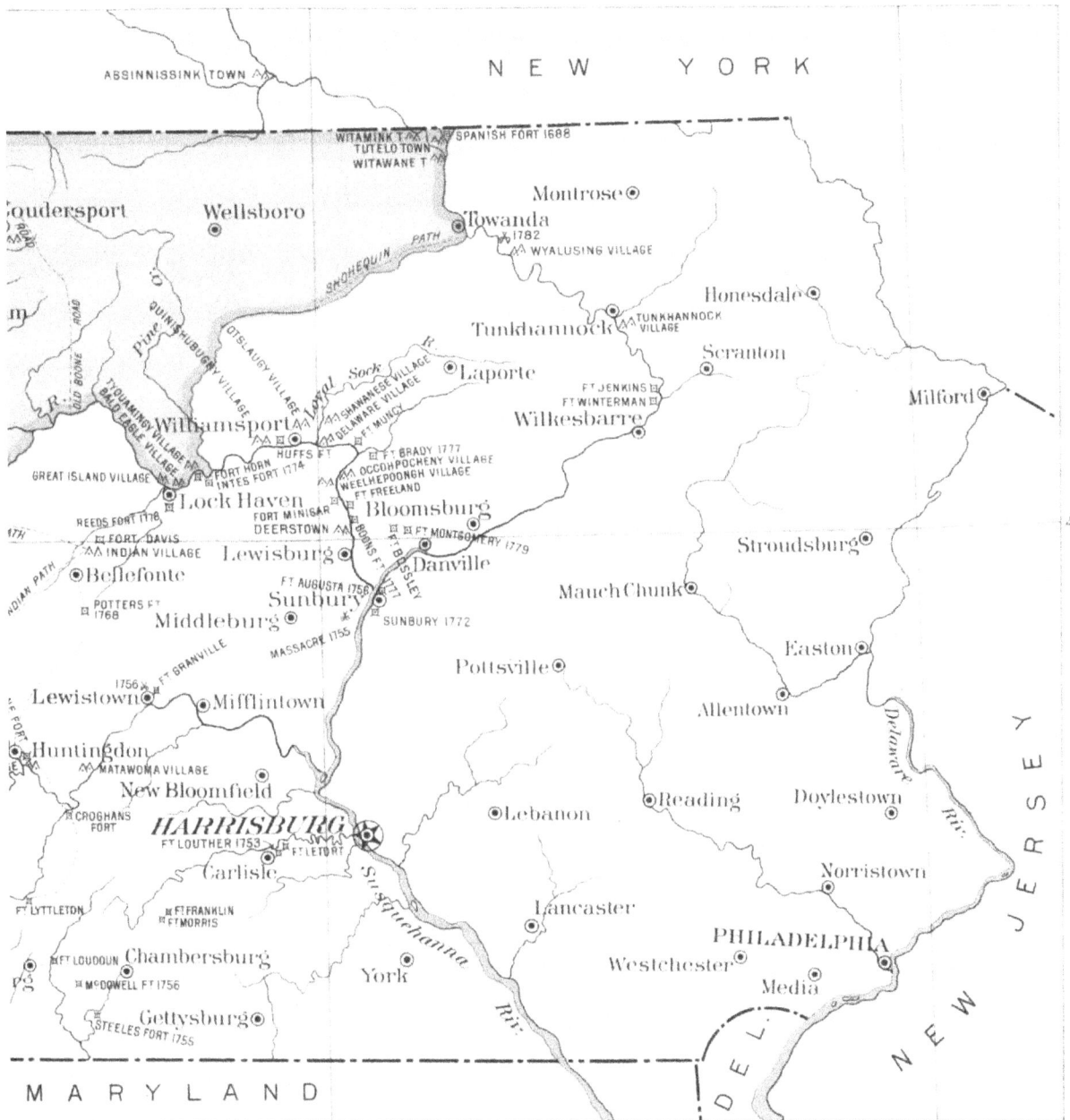

Royce Map of Pennsylvania - East

Pennsylvania Place Names

Pennsylvania has no federally-recognized or state-recognized Tribes.
Notations used: p.n. = place name; t.s. = treaty signer; and ntg = no translation given.

Allegheny: from Kithanne: Main Stream

Carlisle: home of the United States Indian Industrial School; this was the flagship Indian boarding school in the US from 1879 through 1918

Conoy: from Guneu: Long

Delaware River: was originally called Lenape Wihittuck: River of the Lenape, or Maksrick-kitton: Large River

Erie: Cougar (or Panther) Place; or (less likely) from Yenrash: It Is Long-tailed, or Panther

Genesee: from Gennesheyo: Beautiful Valley

Juniata: from Tyunayate: Projecting Rock

Kittanning: At the Big River, or Town on the Great River

Lackawanna: from Lechauhannek: Forks of the Stream

Lehigh: from Lechauwekink: At the Falls, or from Lechauweeki: Where There Are Forks

Lenape: Men of Our Nation, or Real People

Lycoming: from Legauihanne: Sandy Stream, or from Legawing: At the Place of Sand

Macungy: Feeding Place of Bears

Mahanoy: Salt Lick

Mahoning: At the Salt Lick

Manhattan: Hilly Island, or Bow and Arrow Wood Place

Maxatawny: Bear Path, or Bear's Path Stream

Mexico (from the Aztec): Place of the War God

Monongahela: River Digging Away Its Shores, or River with Sliding Banks; or from Menaun-gehilla: River with Banks that Fall Down

Nanticoke: Tide-water

Neshannock: Double Stream

Ohio: White (see Ohio for complete discussion)

Osceola: Black Drink Hallower

Paxton Creek: from Pekstank: Creek with Pool

Philadelphia: orig. Kuweukwanaku: Tall Pine Grove

Pittsburgh: orig. Menachksink: Where There Is a Fort

Pocohontas: Little Frolic

Pocono: Valley Stream

Poconos: from Pohopoko: Two Mountains with Stream Between

Punxsutawney: Gnat Place, or Sand-fly Town

Schuylkill: Hidden River (perhaps a Dutch word and not Native at all); orig. Ganshowehanne: Roaring Stream, or Noisy Stream Flowing Over

Shamokin: Eel Place

Shenandoah: Very Great Plain, Spruce Stream, or Beautiful Daughter of the Stars

Shenango: Beautiful One

Susquehanna: Muddy River; or from Guneshachachgak-hanne: Great Bend River

Tamarack: from Hackmatack: Bad Lowlands (that is, the place where these trees grow)

Tioga: Peaceful Valley, Place of Entrance (or The Gate), Place Between Two Points, or At the Forks

Towanda: Burial Place

Tunkhannock: Small Stream

Venango: Figure Carved on a Tree

Wheeling Creek: from Wihling: Place of the Head

Wyoming: from M'chevomi: Extensive Flats

Ciricahua Apaches at the Carlisle Indian School, Penna., circa 1885,
as they looked upon arrival at the School.
Image courtesy of Library of Congress.

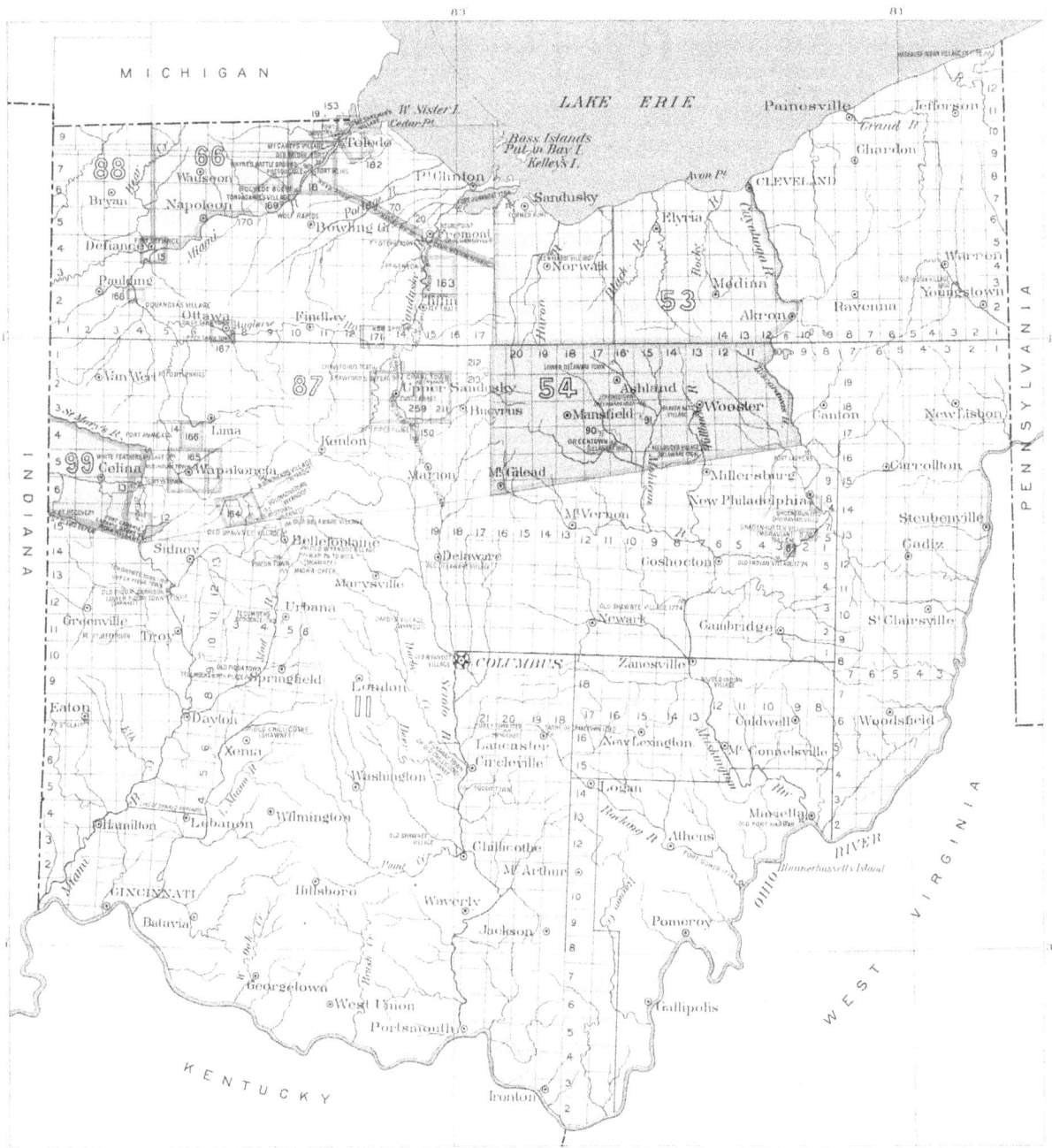

Royce Map of Ohio

Ohio Place Names

OHIO – or Large River, or Fair to Look Upon, or simply Beautiful; other sources claim that the word is only a prefix meaning White Caps (or simply White). The full word for the river should then be Ohio-pek-hanne: River Whitened By Froth; or Ohiophanne: River Full of White Caps, or Very White River; also a CO, IL, IN, KY, NY, PA, WV place name.

Ohio has no federally-recognized or state-recognized Tribes.
Notations used: p.n. = place name; t.s. = treaty signer; and ntg = no translation given.

Ashtabula: Many Fish River, or Always Enough Fish Moving in the River

Chattanooga: Rock Rising to a Point

Chillicothe: Village

Coshocton: Union of Waters, or Black Bear Town

Cuyahoga: Important River, Crooked, or Lake River

Erie: Long-tailed, or Panther; PA p.n.; NY p.n.; OH p.n.; on p.n.

Gahanna: Three Creeks Joining into One. OH p.n.

Geauga: Racoon

Gnadenhutten: Moravian mission site of the slaughter of 90+ unarmed "Praying Indians" on March 8, 1782, by Pensylvania "militiamen."

Huron: named after the Tribe (French origin, with uncertain meaning)

Mahoning: Salt Lick

Maumee: People of the Peninsula

Mexico: from the Aztec: Place of the War God

Miami: Peninsula People

Mississinewa: Big Stone River

Muskingum: By the River

Pataskala: from Pat-aaps-ku-lu: Up To a Point Always a Swell Exists; OH p.n.

Peoria: Carriers

Pickaway: Ashes Men (ie, they rose from ashes)

Sandusky: At the Cold Water, or Pure Water Source

Scioto: Deer

Seneca: from the tribal name; OH p.n.

Tappan: Cold Stream

Tippecanoe: Buffalo Fish

Tuscarawas: Open Mouth

Wyandotte: Islanders, or Peninsula Dwellers

MASSACRE OF THE CHRISTIAN INDIANS.

On March 8, 1782, a group of Pennsylvania militiamen slaughtered some 90 unarmed Christian
"Praying Indians" at the Moravian mission settlement of Gnadenhutten, Ohio.
Image courtesy of Library of Congress.

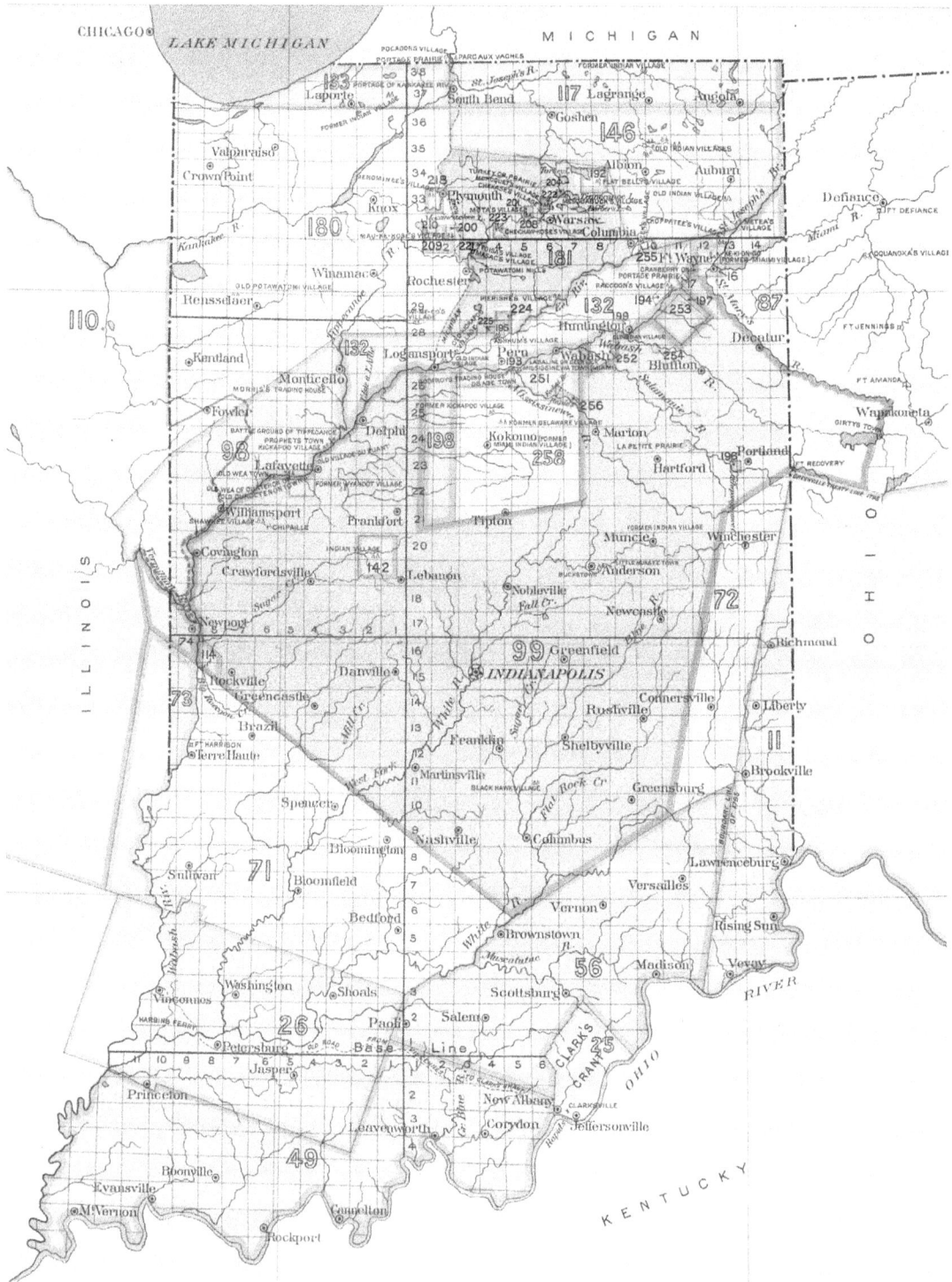

Royce Map of Indiana

Indiana Place Names

INDIANA - obvious source of its name is from its indigenous inhabitants.

Indiana has no federally-recognized or state-recognized Tribes

Notations used: p.n. = place name; t.s. = treaty signer; and ntg = no translation given.

Cayuga: from Gaw Ugwck: Where They Take the Boats Out

Detroit River: aka Wahweahtunong (ntg)

Elkhart: from Mesheh-wehoudehik: Elk Heart (from an island of this shape)

Genesee: Beautiful Valley

Kanakee: from Tehyakkeki: Lowland, or Swampy Country

Kokomo: Black Walnut, or The Diver

Maumee: from Meahme: All Friends

Miami: from Oumaumeg: Peninsula People, or from Wemiamik: All Friends

Mishawaka: from M'sehwahkeeki: Country of Dead Trees

Modoc: from Shasteeca word for Enemy

Muncie: Stone Country People

Muscatatuck: Clear River

Ohio: White; the river should be Ohio-pek-hanne: River Whitened By Froth.

Owasco: Floating Bridge

Salamonie: Yellow Paint

Shakanak: Slippery Fish (eel)

Tippacanoe (also spelled Tippecanoe elsewhere): from Ketapekonnong: Buffalo Fish Place

Topeka: Good Potato Place (from the Shawnee word for Jerusalem Artichoke)

Wabash: Bog River, White Water, or Pure White (in reference to its limestone bed)

Winona: First-Born Daughter

Yellow River: from Waythowkahmik: Yellow Waters

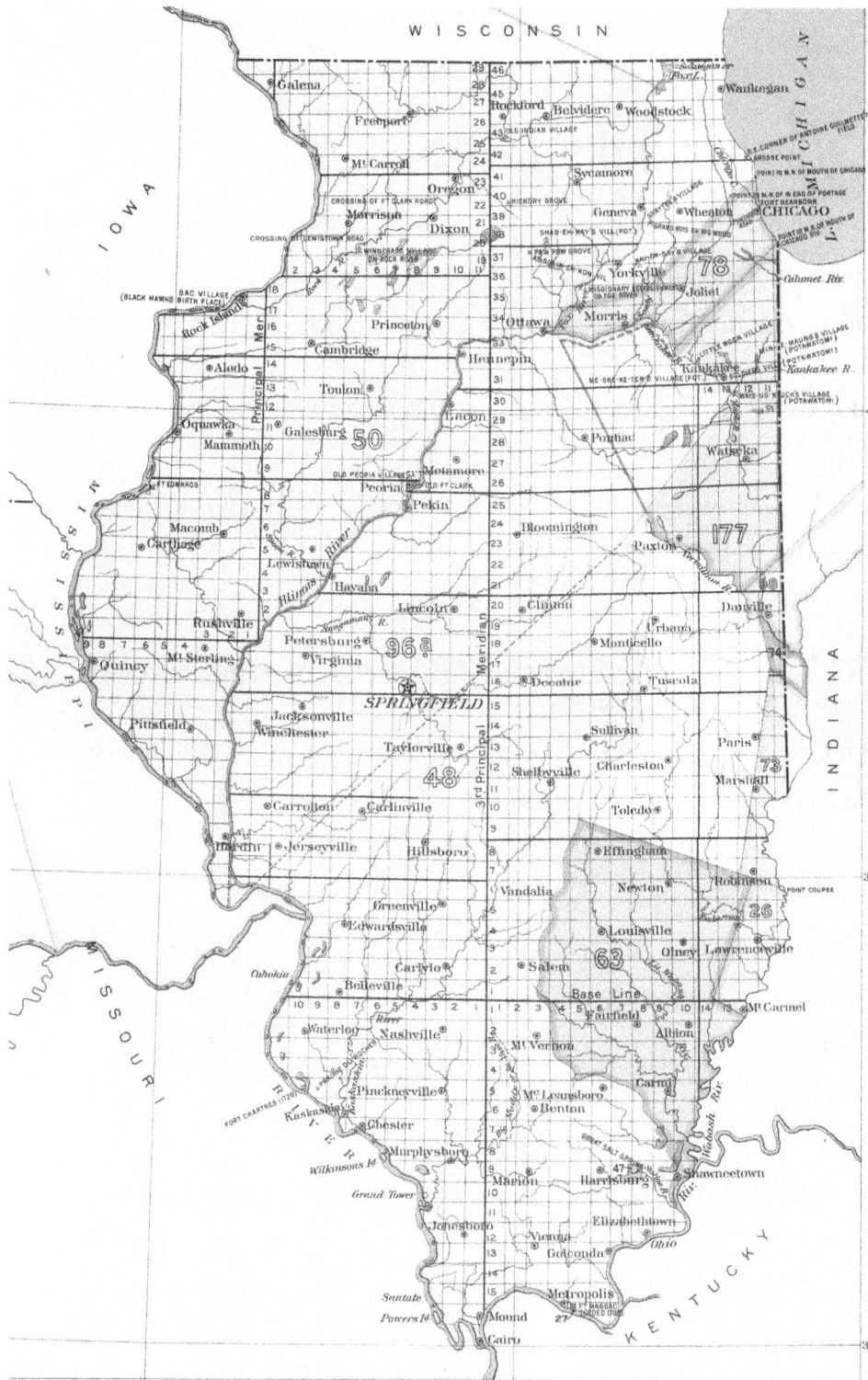

Royce Map of Illinois - 1

Royce Map of Illinois -2

Illinois Place Names

ILLINOIS - from Illini: Man; plural, Illiniwok: People, or Perfect and Accomplished Men.

Illinois has no federally-recognized or state-recognized Tribes

Notations used: p.n. = place name; t.s. = treaty signer; and ntg = no translation given.

Aptakisic: Halfday, or Sun at the Center of the Sky

Chebance: Little Duck

Chicago: several possibilities: from Chicacwa: Garlic, Onion, Leek, Onion Place, or Garlic Field; or from Jikagons: Skunk, Polecat Place, or Kitten Skunk Place

Chillicothe: Village

Erie: Long Tail

Genesee (or Genesco): Shining Valley, or Beautiful Valley

Kankakee: Crow, or Wolf Land

Kansas: South Wind

Kewanee: Greater Prairie Chicken

Kishwaukee: Sycamore River

Mackinaw: Turtle

Maquon: Mussel, or Mussel Shell

Macoupin: Potato

Macoupin: White Potato

Mendota: Junction of Two Trails

Merrimac: Place of Strong Current

Minonk: Good Place

Mokena: Mud Turtle

Neoga: Deer

Nokomis: Grandmother

Oswego: Outpouring

Panola: Cotton

Pecatonica: Slow Water

Peoria: from Piwarea; He Comes Carrying a Pack on His Back, or simply, Carriers

Pistakee (Highlands): Buffalo Place

Potomac: Where Goods Are Brought In

Saganashkee (Slough): Slush of the Earth

Sangamon: Outlet, or Plenty to Eat Land

Sauk: Yellow Earth People

Scioto: Deer

Sinsinawa: Home of the Young Eagle

Skokie: Marsh

Tioga: Peaceful Valley, or At the Forks

Tekakwitha (Kateri): One Who Puts Things in Order, or She Hesitates; aka The Lily of the Mohawks; Mohawk spiritual woman beatified by the Roman Catholic church in 2012; 1656-1680.

Topeka: Good Potato Place

Towanda: Burial Place

Wabash: Bog River, Color-bright, Pure White, or White Water

Walla Walla: Many Waters

Watseka: Daughter of the Evening Star

Waukegan: Sheltering Place, Fort, or Trading Post

Wauponsee: Bright Place in the Sky

Winnebago: a tribal name (see entry in alphabetical listing for meanings)

Winnetka: Beautiful Place

Wyoming: At the Smaller River Hills

Royce Map of Wisconsin

Wisconsin Place Names

WISCONSIN: possible source is Weeskonsan: Gathering of the Waters, Muskrat Land, or Grassy Place; or from Meskousing: Where the Waters Gather, Place of the Red Earth People, or Red Stone; or from Misconsin: Strong Current.

Notations used: p.n. = place name; t.s. = treaty signer; and ntg = no translation given.

Bad River: from Masshki-zeebi, but it is said that it was originally Maski Sebi: Swamp River; ("maski" was mistook for "matchi," so we get Bad, not Swamp)

Brothertown Indian Nation: landless, but most live in the Fond du Lac region

Cedar Point: aka Keshegekiaktakewum: Cedar Ridge

Chequamegon: from Shaugauwaumekong: Long Narrow Strip of Land Running Into the Water

Chicago: from Chicacwa: Garlic, or Onion, or Leek

Chipmunk: Ojibway for squirrel

Chippecotton: Root (now called Racine)

Chippewa: Voice Gathered Up, or Puckered Voice (see Ojibway, p.99, for complete discussion)

Door County: orig. Kenatao: Cape

Eau Claire: French for Clear Water: from Wayaconuttaquayaw Sebe: Water (of the River) Is Clear

Forest County Potawatomi: Reservation

Genesee: from Gennesheyo: Beautiful Valley

Gogebic: On the Rock, or Green Lake

Green Bay: orig. Pujikut: Bay in Spite of Everything

Ho-Chunk Nation: formerly the Winnebago; Reservation

Horicon: Silver Water

Kaukauna: from Okakaning: Fishing Place, or Crow-nesting Place, or Long Portage

Kenosha: Pickerel, or Pike

Keshena: Swift Flying Hawk

Kewaunee: from Kakiweonan: Land Crossing By Boat; or To Cross a Point, Prairie Hen, or Wild Duck

Kickapoo: He Moves About

Kinnickinnic: It Is Mixed (a smoking mixture of tobacco, sumac, and red willow)

Kiwanis: Noise, or Noisy

Koshkonong: Closed in By Fog, or Hog Place

La Pointe: orig. Moningwonaekauning: Lapwing (or Plover) Land

Lac Courte Oreilles (Band of Lake Superior Chippewa): Lake of the Short Ears; Reservation

Lac du Flambeau: Lake of Torches; Reservation

Madeline Is.: orig. Moningwunkaning: Lapwing Place, or Golden-breasted Woodpecker Place; renamed after Chief White Crane's daughter

Madison: orig. Dejop: Four Lakes

Manitowoc: Spirit Land, or River of Bad Spirits

Mdewakanton Sioux: Lower Sioux Indian Community; Reservation

Menasha: Thorn in the Island

Mendota: Mouth of the River, River Junction, or Lake Outlet

Menominee (Indian Tribe): Wild Rice; self-designation is Mamaceqtaw – The People; Reservation

Merrimac: Fish (sturgeon or catfish)

Milwaukee: from Mene-awkee; Good Earth, or Rich Land; or from Mino-aki: Fair, Fertile Land

Missabe (Iron Range): Giant

Mole Lake (Band of Lake Superior Chippewa): Sokaogon (Chippewa Community): Post in the Lake; WI Reservation

Mosinee: Moose

Mukwonago: Bend in the Stream

Namekagon: Sturgeon Place

Necedah: Yellow

Neenah: Running Water

Neosho: Cold, Clear Water, or Main River

Niagara: Neck of Land Between Lakes

Oconomowoc: River of Lakes, or Waterfall

Oconto: Pike (or Pickerel) Place, or River of Plentiful Fish

Ojibway: Puckered Up (see Ojibway, p.99, for complete discussion)

Oneida: People of the Standing Stone; Reservation

Ontario: Great Lake, or Beautiful Lake

Osceola: Black Drink Hallower; Seminole; c1803-1838

Oshkosh: Hoof, Claw, Nail; Menominee; 1795-1858

Oswego: Flowing Out (as a river into a lake)

Otsego: Place of the Rock

Outagamie: Dwellers on the Other Side

Ozaukee: Mouth of the River, or Yellow Earth Place

Peshtigo: Snapping Turtle, or Wild Goose

Pewabik: Iron

Prairie du Chien: named after Fox chief known as Dog

Quinnesec Falls: Where It Is Noisy, or Smoke (in reference to mist from falls)

Red Cliff (Band of Lake Superior Chippewa): Gaa-Miskwaabikaang: Place of Red Rock Cliffs; Reservation

Rockaway: from Rechouwhacky: Sandy Land

Saint Croix Chippewa Indians of Wisconsin; Reservation

Sandusky: Pure Water, or Cool Water

Saratogo: Beaver Place

Sauk: from Osaukie-uck: Yellow Earth People

Shawano: To the South

Sheboygan: Needle, Awl, Disappearing River, Noise Underground, Reed-Like, Thundering Under the Ground, or Something that Pierces; or from Shabwawagoning: Rumbling Waters, or Waters Disappearing Underground

Stockbridge-Munsee: an amalgamated tribe of Stockbridge people made up of Mahican and other, and the Munsee who are a Delaware subgroup. Moved by the government to Wisconsin from the northeast in the 1840s. WI tribe, Reservation

Tekakwitha (Kateri): One Who Puts Things in Order, or She Hesitates; Mohawk holy woman made a Saint by the Catholic Church in 2012; 1656-1680

Thunder Mtn.: from Chequah Bikwaki

Waukesha: from Wakusheg: Foxes, or Little Foxes; or Burnt, Fire-land

Waunakee: Spirit (Departed from a Body)

Waupaca: Clear Water Place, or Brave Young Hero

Waupun: East, Daybreak, or Dawn

Wausau: Far Away

Wausaukee: Far Away Land

Waushara: Good Land River, Big Fox, or Foxes

Weyauwega: Here We Rest

White Earth (Reservation): Gaa-waabaabiganikaag: Place of White Clay

Winnebago: People of the Filthy Waters

Wisconsin Dells: orig. Neechahkekoonahonah: Where the Rocks Strike Together

Native Americans, possibly Winnebago, on rocks at the Dells of the Wisconsin, c. 1925.
Image courtesy of Library of Congress.

Royce Map of Minnesota

Minnesota Place Names

MINNESOTA - several possible meanings: Sky-colored, Whitish, or Milky Water; Water Reflecting Cloudy Skies; Reflection of Sky on Water; or Land of Many Lakes.

Notations used: p.n. = place name; t.s. = treaty signer; and ntg = no translation given.

Anoka: The Other Side, or Both Sides

Bemidji: River Crossing Lake

Bois Forte (Band of Chippewa): Strong Wood; Reservation

Chanhassen: Tree with Sweet Juice

Chaska: First-born Son

Chippewa: tribal name; (see Ojibway, p. 99, for complete discussion)

Chisago: from, Kichisaga: Large and Lovely Lake, Large and Beautiful, or Large and Fair

Cloquet: orig. Pashkoninitigong: Barren Place

Crow Wing: from Kagiwigwan: Crow (or Raven's) Wing, or Raven Feather

Dakota: tribal name; aka Sioux

Fond du Lac: from Wanikamiu: End of the Lake; Reservation

Gichi-Onigaing: Grand Portage (Band of Lake Superior Chippewa); Reservation

Grand Marais: orig. Kitchi-bitobigong: Great Pond Place

Grand Portage: Kitchi-Winigumeeng

Isanti: Dwelling At Knife Lake

Ishtakhaba: Sleepy Eyes; after the Sisseton Dakota leader of the late 1800s

Kanabec: Snake

Kandiyohi: Buffalo Fish Come, or Where the Buffalo Fish Arrive

Keewatin: North Wind Place

Koochiching: Rainy Lake

Lake Itasca: source of Mississippi; not of Native origin; given Indian-sounding name by Indian Agent Henry Rowe Schoolcraft, from the Latin, verITAS CAput: "In Truth, The Head"

Leech Lake: from Gasagaskwajimekang: There Are Leeches There, or Full of Leeches

Mahnomen: Wild Rice

Makato River: from Makato Osa Watapa: River Where Blue Earth Is Gathered

Mankato: Blue Earth, or Earth Paint Pigment; site of largest mass execution in U.S. history, where 38 Dakota Sioux were hanged on Dec. 26, 1862.

38+2 -- THOSE HUNG AT MANKATO, MINNESOTA, DECEMBER 26, 1862.

Aichaga: To Grow Upon

Amdacha: Broken to Pieces

Baptiste Campbell: (French mixed-blood)

Cetan-hunka: The Parent Hawk

Chanka-hdo: Near the Woods

Dan Little: Chaska-dan: family name for a first son (this may be We-chank-wash-ta-don-pee, who had been pardoned and was mistakenly executed when he answered to a call for "Chaska")

Dowan-niye: The Singer

Had-hin-hda: To Make a Rattling Noise

Hapinkpa: Tip of the Horn

Henry Milord: (French mixed-blood)

Hepan: (family name for a second son)

Hepidan: (family name for a third son)

Hinhan-shoon-koyag-mani: Walks Clothed in an Owl's Tail

Ho-tan-inku: Voice Heard in Returning

Hypolite Auge (French mixed-blood)

Ite-duta: Scarlet Face

Maka-te-najin: Stands Upon Earth

Marpiya-te-najin: Stands on a Cloud (Cut Nose)

Maza-bomidu: Iron Blower

Mehu-we-mea: He Comes for Me

Nape-shuha: Does Not Flee

Oyate-tonwan: The Coming People

Pazi-kuta-mani: Walks Prepared to Shoot

Radapinyanke: Rattling Runner

Sna-mani: Tinkling Walker

Taju-xa: Red Otter

Tate-hdo-dan: Wind Comes Back

Tate-kage: Wind Maker

Tipi-hdo-niche: Forbids His Dwelling

Tunkan-icha-ta-mani: Walks With His Grandfather

Tunkan-koyag-i-najin: Stands Clothed with His Grandfather

Wahena: translation unknown

Wakanozanzan and **Shakopee:** These two chiefs who fled north after the war, were kidnapped from Canada in January 1864 and were tried and convicted in November that year and their executions were approved by President Andrew Johnson (after Lincoln's assassination) and they were hanged November 11, 1865.

Wakan-tanka: Great Spirit

Wakinyan-na: Little Thunder

Wapa-duta: Scarlet Leaf

Waxicun-na: Little Whiteman (this young white man, adopted by the Dakota at an early age and who was acquitted, was hanged, nevertheless).

Wyata-tonwan: His People

Xunka-ska: White Dog

Mendota: River Junction, or Lake Outlet

Mesabi: Giant, or Hidden Giant (Iron Range name)

Mille Lacs (Band of Ojibwe): Thousand Lakes (French); aka **Misi-zaaga'igan:** Grand Lake; Reser-vation

Minneapolis: Water (or Waterfall) City: from the Sioux 'Minne' plus the Greek 'apolis' (city)

Minnetonka: Big Water

Missabe: Giant, or Hidden Giant

Nashua: Beautiful River with Pebbly Bottom

Ponemah: One Stops Talking To Another

Prairie Island Indian Community: Mdewakanton Sioux Reservation

Red Lake (Band of Chippewa Indians): Miskwaagamiiwi-zaaga'iganing; Reservation

Red Wing: from Koopoohoosha: Wing of the Wild Swan Dyed Scarlet

Shakopee (Mdewakanton Dakota Community); Six (hereditary name); Reservation

Upper Sioux Community: aka Pejuhutazzi Kapi: Place To Dig for Yellow Medicine; Reservation

Wabasha: Red Leaf, or Red Battle-standard

Wadena: Little Round Hill

Waseca: Rich, or Fertile (soil)

Watonwan: Fish Bait Place, or Where Fish Abound

White Earth Reservation: aka Gawababiganikag: White Clay, or Gawababigunikag Sagaiigun: White Clay Place

Winnebago: tribal name; Fish Eaters, or People of the Sea

Winona: First Born (if a daughter)

Yellow Medicine: from; Pezhihutazizi Kapi: Diggings of Yellow Plant Root (Moonseed)

As a result of the Sioux Uprising in 1862, 392 prisoners were tried, 303 were sentenced to death, and 16 were given prison terms. After a review of their death-sentence convictions by President Lincoln, many convictions were reversed, and on December 26, 1862, 38 Dakota men were hanged at Mankato, the largest mass execution in US history.
Image courtesy of Library of Congress.

Alphabetical Listing of Indian Names

Notations used: p.n. = place name; t.s. = treaty signer; and ntg = no translation given.

- 𝒜 -

Aamjiwnaang: At the Spawning Stream; First Nation of Ontario

Abetang: He Who Inhabits; 1866 t.s. Ojibway notable.

Abitibi: Half-way Water (in reference to trading posts in either direction). ON p.n.

Absconder: Hodegweh; aka Orris Farmer; 19th c. Onondaga notable.

Accomplished Men --Illinois - from Illini: Man; plural, Illiniwok: People, or Perfect and Accomplished Men; Illinois divisions: Cahokia (ntg), and Tamaroa: He Has a Cut Tail; Oklahoma tribe

Acqueweezais: Expert Boy, or Wickedly Expert; 1837 t.s. Ojibway notable.

Adaquarande (ntg); aka Sadekanakte (ntg); 1640-1701. Onondaga notable.

Adawawnequabenace: Twin-haired Bird; 1866 t.s. Ojibway notable.

Adawe or Odahwe, preferred pronounciation of OTTAWA: most often translated as Traders, To Trade (or Barter), or Bartering Place; it may also mean To Sell (not trade); preferred; possible source is from Odauwau-ininiwuk, meaning Bullrush People; self-desig. Anishnabeg: Original People; part of the Three Fires Confederacy; Ottawa divisions, Kiskakon: Cut Tails, or Bear Clan; Nassauaketon: People of the Fork; Sable: Sandy Country People; Sinago: Squirrel Clan; Michigan, Oklahoma, Ontario tribe; IL, KS, MI, NWT, OH, OK, Ont., Que., WV p.n.

Adawegeshik (or Adawwegezhick): Both Ends of the Sky, or Each Side of the Day; 1837, 1854 t.s. Ojibway notable.

Agawa Canyon: Bending Shore. ON p.n.

Ahahjawwakeshick: Crossing Sky; 1863 t.s. Ojibway notable.

Ahooshushkah: Red Wing; 1837 t.s. Winnebago notable.

Ahsheeshkaw: Broken Arm; 1829 t.s. Winnebago notable.

Aishkebogekoshe: Flat Mouth; 1837, 1847, 1855 t.s. Ojibway notable.

Akwesasne: Land Where the Partridge Drums; aka St. Regis Reservation. Ontario First Nation, New York Reservation.

Alderville: First Nation of Ontario

Algonkian; aka Stockbridge-Munsee; an amalgamated tribe of Stockbridge people made up of Mahican and other, and the Munsee who are a Delaware subgroup. Moved by the government to Wisconsin from the northeast in the 1840s. WI tribe.

Algonkin: Fish Spearing Place. Ontario Tribe/First Nation.

Algonquin: Spearing Fish from the End of a Canoe, or Spearing Fish Place. ON p.n.

Algonquins of Pikwàkanagàn: A Hilly Place; First Nation of Ontario

All Around the Sky: Kewetakepe; 1825 t.s. Ojibway

All Friends, from Meahme: Maumee. IN p.n.

Allegheny: from Kithanne: Main Stream. PA p.n.

Along the Water's Edge, or Continuous Water: Animibeegoong; aka Nipigon: So Long that You Cannot See the End of It. ON p.n.

Alpena: County given "Indian-sounding" name by Indian Agent Henry Rowe Schoolcraft, possibly meant to refer to the Partridge. MI p.n.

Always Enough Fish Moving in the River: Ashtabula, or Many Fish River, OH p.n.

Always Plenty of Game, or River of Short Bends and Many Islands: Kakabeka Falls. ON p.n.

American: Chemokcomon (literally, Long Knife); 1817 t.s. Ojibway notable.

Angling Lake: former name for Wapekeka (ntg) First Nation (Ontario)

Anibiminani Zibi Wininiwug: High-bush Cranberry River People: Pembina; Ojibway band.

Animbiigoo Zaagi'igan Anishinaabek (ntg); First Nation of Ontario

Animibeegoong: Along the Water's Edge, or Continuous Water; aka Nipigon: So Long that You Cannot See the End of It. ON p.n.

Animikie Wekwed: Thunder Bay; orig. Gamanautigawaeyauk: Land of Many River Islands. ON p.n.

Anishinaabeg of Naongashiing: Big Island; First Nation of Ontario

Anishinabek: Original People, or Those Who Intend To Do Well; self-desig. of the Ojibway (Chip-pewa), Ottawa, and Potawatomi. Great Lakes Tribal People.

Anoka: The Other Side, or Both Sides. MN p.n.

Aptakisic: Halfday; IL p.n.

Archsisorihenn: He is to Blame; aka Solomon, Alexander; 19th c. leader. Mohawk notable.

Armstrong; aka Pamozet (ntg); 1805 t.s. Munsee notable.

Aroland: First Nation of Ontario

Aseanse: Little Shell; 1863 t.s. Ojibway notable.

Aseenewub: Little Rock; 1863, 1864 t.s. Ojibway notable.

Ashes Men (ie, they rose from ashes): Pickaway. OH p.n.

Ashtabula: Many Fish River, or Always Enough Fish Moving in the River. OH p.n.

Assembly: Cabamabee; 1825 t.s. Ojibway notable.

Assiginack (Jean Baptiste): Blackbird; 1768-1866. Ottawa notable.

Asubpeeschoseewagong: (ntg) First Nation; formerly known as Grassy Narrows (Ontario)

At the Big River, or Town on the Great River: Kittanning. PA p.n.

At the Cold Water: Sandusky, or Pure Water Source. OH p.n.

At the Edge of a Whirlpool, Narrows Separating Two Lakes, or Group of Pine Trees: Couchiching. Ontario First Nation.

At the Falls: Lechauwekink; source of Lehigh; or from Lechauweeki: Where There Are Forks. PA p.n.

At the Forks, or Place Between Two Points, or Peaceful Valley, or Place of Entrance (or The Gate): Tioga. PA p.n.

At the Mouth of the River: Zaagiing; source of Saugeen First Nation (Ontario)

At the Place Where the Current is Obstructed: Naicatchewenin First Nation (Ontario)

At the Salt Lick: Mahoning. PA p.n.

At the Spawning Stream: Aamjiwnaang; First Nation of Ontario

Atiatoharongwen: His Body Is Taken Down from Hanging, or One Who Pulls Down the People; aka Louis Cook; c1740-1814. Mohawk notable.

Atikameksheng Anishnawbek: (ntg) formerly known as the Whitefish Lake First Nation (of Ontario)

Atikokan: Caribou Bone. ON p.n.

Attawapiskat: Rock Bottom. ON p.n.

Attawapiskat: First Nation of Ontario

Attempter: Kaygwadaush; 1855 t.s. Ojibway notable.

Aughquanahquose: Stumptail Bear; 1814 t.s. Ottawa notable.

Aumidjiwunaung: Place Where the Waters Collect: original name for Sarnia. ON p.n.

Awawbedwaywedung: Returning Echo; 1863 t.s. Ojibway notable.

Awdekonse: Little Reindeer; 1854 t.s. Ojibway notable.

Awkewainze: Old Man; 1854 t.s. Ojibway notable.

Awl, Needle, Disappearing River, Noise Underground, Reed-Like, Thundering Under the Ground, or Something that Pierces: Sheboygan; or from Shabwawagoning: Rumbling Waters, or Waters Disappearing Underground. WI p.n. Cheboygan; MI p.n.

Awmose: Wasp; 1854 t.s. Ojibway notable.

Aztec; from Mexico: Place of the War God. OH p.n.

- *B* -

Baagwaashiing: Where the Water is Shallow; aka Pays Plat (French: Flat Land); First Nation of Ontario

Babaseekundade: Curling Hair; 1825 t.s. Ojibway notable.

Babawmadjeweshcang: Mountain Traveler; 1866 t.s. Ojibway notable.

Bad Bird: Mashipinashiwish; 1795 t.s. Ojibway notable.

Bad Bird: Match-e-be-nash-she-wish (Band of Pottawatomi Indians); aka Gun Lake Tribe; Michi-gan Reservation

Bad Boy: Quewesansish (various spellings); 1854, 1855, 1863, 1864, 1867 t.s. Ojibway notable.

Bad Boy: Weweshanshis; aka Big Mouth; 1837 t.s. Ojibway notable.

Bad Legs: Mamaushegauta; 1807 t.s. Ojibway notable notable.

Bad Lowlands: Hackmatack: (that is, the place where these trees grow); source of Tamarack. PA p.n.

Bad River; the Ojibway term is Maski Sipi (swamp river) which was mistaken for Matchi Sipi (bad river), so it is claimed that it should be Swampy River. WI reservation; WI p.n.

Bagoonakeezhig: Hole in the Day: 1837 t.s. Ojibway notable.

Bald Eagle: Keueaghbon; 1818 t.s. Ottawa notable.

Ball, The: Poquaquet; 1807 t.s. Ojibway notable.

Balsom: Shinggoope; 1854 t.s. Ojibway notable.

Banks, Dennis; aka Nowacumig: At the Center of the Universe; co-founder of the American Indian Movement. 1937-2017. Ojibway notable.

Bare West Place: Mitchigee-waedinong: aka West Bay (Manitoulin Is). Ontario First Nation.

Barren Place: Cloquet; orig. Pashkoninitigong. MN p.n.

Bartering Place, To Trade: Ottawa; Basil Johnston, an Ojibway speaker, says the word means To Sell, not To Trade; he also says that the Ottawa River is named from Odauwuhnshk, which means Bullrush River. ON p.n.

Bastard: Kemenechagon; 1815 t.s. Ottawa notable.

Batchewana: (ntg); First Nation of Ontario

Batchewana Bay: Welling Waters Place. ON p.n.

Bauzhi-geezhig-waeshikum: One Who Steps Over the Sky; Ojibway notable. ?-1841.

Baweting: Gathering Place of the People, Place of the Rapids, or River Beaten to a Spray, original name for Sault Ste. Marie. MI p.n. ON p.n.

Bay in Spite of Everything: Pujikut; original name for Green Bay; orig. WI p.n.

Bay in the Lake, or Opening: Kanitareonto; possible source of Toronto: Fallen Trees in the Water, or Meeting Place; or from Deondo: Trees Growing Out of the Water; or from Thorontohen: Timbers on the Water. ON p.n.

Bay Mills; orig. Ginozhaekaunning: Pike Place. Michigan reservation.

Bay of Gray Slate: Sheguiandah First Nation (Ontario)

Bear Cub: Mecosta. MI p.n.

Bear Island People; aka Teme-agama Anishnabay. Ontario Tribe/First Nation.

Bear Path, or Bear's Path Stream: Maxatawny. PA p.n.

Bear Who Scratches: Mennekam; 1829 t.s. Winnebago notable.

Bear: Nisiwaurooshkun; 1829 t.s. Winnebago notable.

Bear; aka Le Pesant: Heavy; fl. 1703-12. Ottawa notable.

Bearfoot Onondaga: First Nation of Ontario

Bear's Heart: Macouda; 1837 t.s. Ojibway notable.

Bear's Heart: Mawcawday; 1854 t.s. Ojibway notable.

Bear's Legs: Watashnewa; 1814 t.s. Ottawa notable.

Bear's Man: Metesheneiwa; 1818 t.s. Ottawa notable.

Beausoleil: First Nation of Ontario

Beautiful Daughter of the Stars, or Very Great Plain, or Spruce Stream: Shenandoah: PA p.n.

Beautiful Lake: Onitariio; possible source of Ontario; or from Kanadario: Sparkling Water; or from Ontarack: Rocks Standing High in the Water; other possible meanings: Great Lake, Beautiful Lake, Handsome Lake, or Large Lake; NY, OR, WI p.n.

Beautiful One: Shenango. PA p.n.

Beautiful River with Pebbly Bottom: Nashua. MN p.n.

Beautiful River: Ohio ; or Large River, or Fair to Look Upon, or simply Beautiful;

Beautiful Sailor: Wawanosh. ON p.n.

Beautiful Valley: Genesee; possibly from Gennesheyo; IN, MI, PA, WI p.n.

Beaver Bay: Wikwemikong (Manitoulin Is.). Unceded Indian Territory. Ontario First Nation.

Beaver Hat: from Pappellond; 1805 t.s. Munsee notable.

Beaver Place: Saratogo. WI p.n.

Beaverhouse: (non-Status); First Nation of Ontario

Bell: Korokoroheekaw; 1832 t.s. Winnebago notable.

Bell: Tootagen; 1814 t.s. Ottawa notable.

Bemidji: River Crossing Lake. MN p.n.

Bending Shore: Agawa Canyon ON p.n.

Berry Hunter: Cawnawndawwwawwinzo, or Gawnandawawinzo; 1854, 1866 t.s. Ojibway notable.

Berry Hunter: Minduwahwing; 1863 t.s. Ojibway notable.

Besheckkee: Buffalo; 1855, 1863 t.s. Ojibway notable.

Beyond the Swamp: Skanawati; aka John Buck; 19th c. Onondaga keeper of the wampum. Onondaga notable.

Big Bear: Honchhuttakaw; 1855 t.s. Winnebago notable.

Big Bend: Powassan. ON p.n.

Big Bird: Keychepenayse; 1854 t.s. Ojibway notable.

Big Bluffs: Michipicoten First Nation (Ontario)

Big Boat: Watchattykan; 1837 t.s. Winnebago notable.

Big Cloud: Quitchonequit, or Cacheonquet; 1805, 1807, 1815t.s. Ojibway notable.

Big Foot: Maungeezik; 1828 t.s. Winnebago notable.

Big Fox, or Foxes, or Good Land River: Waushara. WI p.n.

Big Frenchman: Kechewametego; 1837 t.s. Ojibway notable.

Big Grassy: First Nation of Ontario

Big Gun: Eezhookhattaykaw, or Shooghattykah; 1832, 1837 t.s. Winnebago notable.

Big Indian: Kacheunishenawbay; 1863 t.s. Ojibway notable.

Big Island: Anishinaabeg of Naongashiing; First Nation of Ontario

Big Lake: Mille Lacs; Mishi-sagaigun: originally the home of the Santee Sioux. MN p.n.

Big Log: Oneida. Ratirontakowa (People of the Big Log) or Onayotekaono (Granite People).

Big Martin: Kechewawbeshayshe; 1854 t.s. Ojibway notable.

Big Medicine Man: Woanknawhoapeenekaw; 1829 t.s. Winnebago notable.

Big Mountain People: Seneca: Tsionontowanehaka, or Nundawaono (Great Hill People) .

Big Mouth; aka Bad Boy: Weweshanshis; 1837 t.s. Ojibway notable.

Big Mouth; Otreouti; fl. 1659-88. Onondaga notable.

Big Outlet (At the): Missaukee. MI p.n.

Big Pipe (People of): Cayuga. Gweugwehono (People at the Mucky Land), or Siotinonawentowane (People of the Big Pipe).

Big Rock, at the: Chesaning. MI p.n.

Big Stone River: Mississinewa. OH p.n.

Big Walker: Mauneehatakau; 1829 t.s. Winnebago notable.

Big Water: Minnetonka. MN p.n.

Big Wave: Tshahtshunhatatykaw; 1832 t.s. Winnebago notable.

Biinjitiwaabik Zaaging Anishinaabek: (ntg); First Nation of Ontario

Bird Forever: Kakekapenais; aka William Pennefeather.

Bird that Flies on One Side: Nabineashe; 1847 t.s. Ojibway notable.

Bird: Paanassee; 1815 t.s. Ojibway notable.

Bisected Bottom Lands, Neck of Land Between Lakes, Thunder of Waters, or Resounding with Great Noise: Niagara; aka Kitchi-Gaugeedjiwunng: Great Falls. ON p.n.

Bitter Body: Hayahdugihwah. aka Thomas Webster, or Joseph Webster. Onondaga; 19th c. keeper of the wampum for the League of the Iroquois. Iroquois notable.

Bkejwanong Territory: Where the Waters Divide; Walpole Island First Nation (Ontario)

Black Bear Town: Coshocton, or Union of Waters. OH p.n.

Black Bird: Sheganack; 1817 t.s. Ojibway notable.

Black Cloud: Mawcawdaywawquot; 1854 t.s. Ojibway notable.

Black Drink Hallower: Osceola. Seminole; c1803-1838. MI. PA, WI p.n.

Black Eagle: Chahwausaipkau; 1829 t.s. Winnebago notable.

Black Hawk: Hayraytshonsarp; 1829 t.s. Winnebago notable.

Black Walnut: Kokomo. or The Diver. IN p.n.

Black Wolf: Shoanktshunksaipkau; 1828, 1829 t.s. Winnebago notable.

Blackbird: Assiginack (Jean Baptiste); 1768-1866. Ottawa notable.

Blue Earth: Mankato: or Earth Paint Pigment (site of largest mass execution in U.S. history, where 38 Dakota Sioux were hanged on Dec. 26, 1862; see list under Mankato, p.42). MN p.n.

Blue Earth: Maushoatshkaw; 1832 t.s. Winnebago notable.

Blue Sky: Ozhawwawscogezhick; 1854 t.s. Ojibway notable.

Bog River: Wabash, or Color-bright, or White Water, or Pure White (in reference to its limestone bed). IL, IN p.n.

Bold Promontories Place, or Broken, Craggy Highlands Place: Michipicoten. ON p.n.

Both Ends of the Sky: Adawegeshik (or Adawwegezhick), or Each Side of the Day; 1837, 1854 t.s. Ojibway notable.

Bouy: Ocundecun; 1854 t.s. Ojibway notable.

Bow and Arrow Wood Place, or Hilly Island: Manhattan. PA p.n.

Bowels (In the): Les Chenaux; orig; Anaminang: In the Bowels (a reference to the channels' tortuous intricacy). MI p.n.

Brant, Beth; aka Degonwadonti: She Who is Outnumbered, or Several Against One; writer, poet; 1941-2015. Mohawk notable.

Brant, Catherine (third wife of Joseph Brant); aka Ohtowa'kehson (ntg); Turtle Clan Mother; c1759-1837. Mohawk notable.

Brant, John: aka Tekarihogen (ntg); youngest son of Joseph Brant; 1794-1832. Mohawk notable.

Brant, Joseph; aka Thayendanegea: He Places Together Two Bets; 1743?-1807. Mohawk notable.

Brant, Mary: aka Konwatsi'tsiaienni: Someone Lends Her a Flower; Clan Mother; c1736-1796. Mohawk notable.

Brant, Molly; aka Degonwadonti: She Who is Outnumbered, or Several Against One; aka Gonwatsijsiaienni: Someone Lends Her a Flower; Mohawk tribal leader; 1736-1796 (sister of Joseph Brant; married to Sir Wm. Johnson, British Indian agent). Mohawk notable.

Bright Light, or Light Falling on a Distant Object: Wasso; 1837 t.s. Ojibway notable.

Brightly Reflecting: Waussaukissing; original name for Parry Island; orig. ON p.n.

Broken Arm: Ahsheeshkaw; 1829 t.s. Winnebago notable.

Broken Arm: Pusisaingegen; 1825 t.s. Ojibway notable.

Broken Chest (or keg, box): Mukkukoosh; 1837 t.s. Ojibway notable.

Broken Tooth: Kautawaubeta; 1825 t.s. Ojibway notable.

Broken, Craggy Highlands Place, or Bold Promontories Place: Michipicoten. ON p.n.

Brunswick House: First Nation of Ontario

Buck, John; aka Skanawati: Beyond the Swamp; 19th c. Onondaga keeper of the wampum. Onondaga notable.

Buffalo Fish Come: from Kandiyohi; or Where the Buffalo Fish Arrive. MN p.n.

Buffalo Fish Place: Tippacanoe. from Ketapekonnong. IN p.n.

Buffalo Fish: Tippecanoe. OH p.n.

Buffalo: Besheckkee; 1855, 1863 t.s. Ojibway notable.

Buffalo: Kechewaishke; 1854 t.s. Ojibway notable.

Buffalo: Peeseeker; 1825 t.s. Ojibway notable.

Buffalo: Pejike; 1847 t.s. Ojibway notable.

Buffalo: Pezheke; 1837 t.s. Ojibway notable.

Buffalo: Waishkey; notable treaty-era chief of the Bay Mills Indian Community; MI p.n. (EUP River). Ojibway notable.

Bugonegijig: Hole in the Day, or Opening in the Sky; 1825-1868. Ojibway notable.

Bullrush People: Odauwau-ininiwuk; possible source of OTTAWA (Page #?)

Bullrush River: Odauwuhnshk; possible source for Ottawa River. ON p.n.

Bun; aka Hotsinonhyahta: Cord (or Sinew); fl. 1748-1774. Onondaga notable.

Burial Place: Towanda. IL, PA p.n.

Burned Over: Kalkaska. MI p.n.

Burning Cloud: from Oronhyatekha; aka Peter Martin; physician, author; 1841-1907. Mohawk notable.

Burt Lake Band of Ottawa and Chippewa Indians: State-recognized Tribe of Michigan.

Button George; aka Sahhugaene (ntg); 1838 t.s. Oneida notable.

Bwaness: Little Shoe; 1864 t.s. Ojibway notable.

Bwondiac: Stopping It (in reference to his warning of an Iroquois raid which saved his village). Aka Pontiac; war chief; 1720-1769. Ottawa notable.

By the River: Muskingum. OH p.n.

Byeajick: Lone Man; 1854 t.s. Ojibway notable.

- C -

Cabamabee: Assembly; 1825 t.s. Ojibway notable.

Cacheonquet: Big Cloud; 1815 t.s. Ojibway notable.

Cachointioni: Red Head; ?-1756. Onondaga notable.

Cagouse: Small Porcupine; 1847 t.s. Ojibway notable.

Cakenjiwinine: Charcoal; 1847 t.s. Ojibway notable.

Caldwell: First Nation of Ontario

Cameron, John; aka Ogimauh-binaessih: Chief Little Bird; aka Wageezhegome: Who Is Like the Day; Mississagua 1764-1828. Ojibway notable.

Cannibals (or Man-Eaters): MOHAWK; possibly from Mohowauuck: They Eat Animate Things Ontario First Nation; NY Tribe.

Cape Croker First Nation (Ontario): now known as the Chippewas of Nawash

Cape Croker; aka Neiyosheonegaming (ntg). Ontario First Nation.

Cape: Kenatao; original name for Door County. WI p.n.

Capemabe: Elder Brother's Son; 1847 t.s. Ojibway notable.

Caribou Bone: Atikokan. ON p.n.

Caricasica: He that Kills the Crow; 1825 t.s. Winnebago notable.

Carimine: Turtle that Walks; 1825 t.s. Winnebago notable.

Carriers: from Piwarea: Peoria. He Comes Carrying a Pack on His Back, or simply, Carriers. IL, OH p.n.

Cat Lake: First Nation of Ontario

Cataraqui: Where River and Lake Meet. ON p.n.

Catfish: Monimack; 1805 t.s. Ojibway notable.

Catfish; Merrimac: Fish (sturgeon or catfish). WI p.n.

Cawcangewegwan: Crow Feather; 1855 t.s. Ojibway notable.

Cawnawndawwawwinzo: Berry Hunter; 1854 t.s. Ojibway notable.

Cawwindow: He that Gathers Berries; 1825 t.s. Ojibway notable.

Cayuga: from Gaw Ugwck: Here They Take the Boats Out. IN, ON p.n., or Where They Take the Boats Out. New York, Ontario Tribe/First Nation.

Cayuga: Gweugwehono (People at the Mucky Land) or Siotinonawentowane (People of the Big Pipe)

Cedar Point; aka Keshegekiaktakewum: Cedar Ridge, or Cedar Point. WI p.n.

Cedar: Shinguax; 1817 t.s. Ojibway notable.

Celestial, or In the Sky: from Garonhiague: aka Ogenheratarihiens: Hot Ash; c1646-1687. Mohawk notable.

Centre of Bird's Tail: Nanawananaw; 1871 "Ojibway/Cree" t.s.

Chaboner; aka Chambly; 1825 t.s. Ottawa notable.

Chahwausaipkau: Black Eagle; 1829 t.s. Winnebago notable.

Chambly; aka Chaboner; 1825 t.s. Ottawa notable.

Changasoning: Nine Fingers; 1847 t.s. Ojibway notable.

Chanhassen: Tree with Sweet Juice. MN p.n.

Chanlyeya: Drifted Snow; aka Joseph Snow; 19th c. Onondaga notable.

Chapleau Cree: First Nation of Ontario

Charcoal: Cakenjiwinine; 1847 t.s. Ojibway notable.

Chaska: First-born Son. MN p.n.

Chattanooga: Rock Rising to a Point. OH p.n.

Cheboygan: Pipe, or Funnel; or from Shabwawagoning: Rumbling Waters, or Waters Disappearing Underground. MI p.n.

Checkered: Mayzin; 1836 t.s. Ojibway notable.

Chejauk: Crane; Ottawa/Ojibway; fl. 1761-1804. Ottawa notable.

Chemokcomon: American (literally, Long Knife); 1817 t.s. Ojibway notable.

Cheonoquet (or Cheanaquod): Great (or Big) Cloud; 1825, 1837 t.s. (see Cacheonquet, above). Ojibway notable.

Chequah Bikwaki: Thunder Mtn. WI p.n.

Chequamegon: from Shaugauwaumekong: Long Narrow Strip of Land Running Into the Water. WI p.n.

Chesaning: At the Big Rock. MI p.n.

Cheyskawkaw: White Ox; 1829 t.s. Winnebago notable.

Chicacwa: Chicago: possibly from Chicacwa: Garlic, Onion, Leek, Onion Place, or Garlic Field; or from Jikagons: Skunk, Polecat Place, or Kitten Skunk Place. IL, WI p.n.

Chicago: possibly from Chicacwa: Garlic, Onion, Leek, Onion Place, or Garlic Field; or from Jikagons: Skunk, Polecat Place, or Kitten Skunk Place. IL, WI p.n.

Chief Little Bird: Ogimauh-binaessih; aka Wageezhegome: Who Is Like the Day; aka John Cameron; Mississagua 1764-1828. Ojibway notable.

Chief of the Earth: Obegwadans; 1837 t.s. Ojibway notable.

Chief of the Mountain: Ogemawwaychewaib; 1863 t.s. Ojibway notable.

Chief Speaker: Ogisna Kegido; 1837 t.s. Ojibway notable.

Chief: Koankaw; 1828 t.s. Winnebago notable.

Chief: Ogemaw. MI p.n.

Chillicothe: Village. IL, OH p.n.

Chipmunk; Ojibway for squirrel. WI p.n.

Chippawa [sic]: People Without Moccasins. ON p.n.

Chippewa of the Thames; First Nation of Ontario

Chippewa, tribal name with various meanings; those found in reference to place names: Gathering Up Voice, Voice Gathered Up, or Puckered Voice.

Chippewa: self-desig. Anishnabek: Original People, Those Who Intend To Do Well, or Great Medicine People. Used inter-changeably with Ojibway, which is translated variously as Those Who Make Pictographs, Talk of the Robin, or Puckered Up. This "Puckered Up" reference is usually associated with either the form of their moccasin seam or their supposed practice of roasting their enemies until they are "puckered up" (which seems a bit ludicrous and does not make linguistic nor historic sense); Chippewa is assumed to be a corruption of Ojibway and is used interchangeably, and in this form its meaning has been given as: Gathering Up Voice, Voice Gathered Up, or Puckered Voice; Chippewa is usually used in the U.S., Ojibway in Canada; The tribe is very extensive and is found in Manitoba, Michigan, Minnesota, Montana, North Dakota, Ontario, Saskatchewan, and Wisconsin. They are part of the Three Fires Confederacy (with the Ottawa and Potawatomi); Ojibway used as place name in MI, MN, MT, WA; the Sioux called them the Hahatonwan: the Camp-at-falls People (a reference to Sault Ste. Marie)

Chippewas of Georgina Island: First Nation of Ontario

Chippewas of Kettle & Stony Point: First Nation of Ontario

Chippewas of Mnjikaning: The Fish Fence at the Narrows; (aka Rama); First Nation of Ontario

Chippewas of Nawash: (formerly known as Cape Croker); First Nation of Ontario

Chippewas of Saugeen: First Nation of Ontario

Chisago: from, Kichisaga: Large and Lovely Lake, Large and Beautiful, or Large and Fair. MN p.n.

Chonquepa: Dog's Head; 1825 t.s. Winnebago notable.

Chorister: Mayajewaywedung; 1855, 1863 t.s. Ojibway notable.

Choukeka: The Ladle; aka Spoon Decora; c1730-1816. Winnebago notable.

Chowwalksaihenic: Plover; 1837 t.s. Winnebago notable.

Claw, Hoof, or Nail: Oshkosh; Menominee; 1795-1858. WI p.n.

Clear River: Muscatatuck. IN p.n.

Clear Round the Prairie: Kaybaishcawdawway; 1854 t.s. Ojibway notable.

Clear Sky (or Clear Weather): Kayrahtshokau; 1828, 1829 t.s. Winnebago notable.

Clear Sky: Eshtonoquot; aka Francis McCoonse; 1836, 1859 t.s. Ojibway notable.

Clear Sky: Wawsaygezhick; 1854 t.s. Ojibway notable.

Clear Water Place: Waupaca. WI p.n.

Cloquet; orig. Pashkoninitigong: Barren Place. MN p.n.

Closed in By Fog, or Hog Place: Koshkonong. WI p.n.

Cloud, Henry Roe; aka Wonaxilayhunka; War Chief; teacher, minister, educator; 1884-1950. Winnebago notable.

Cloudy: Maukeewukkaw; 1832 t.s. Winnebago notable.

Cloudy: Minnesota - with several other translations; Sky-colored, Whitish, or Milky Water; Water Reflecting Cloudy Skies; Reflection of Sky on Water; or Land of Many Lakes.

Coast of the Straits: from Karontaen. Original name for Detroit. Also, Wawiyatanong: Where the River Turns, or Crooked Way; or Yondotiga: Great Village. MI p.n.

Coaticook: River of Pines. ON p.n.

Cockburn Island 19A: former name for Zhiibaahaasing (ntg) First Nation (Ontario)

Cold Stream: Tappan. OH p.n.

Cold, Clear Water, or Main River: Neosho. WI p.n.

Color-bright: Wabash: or Bog River, Color-bright, or White Water. IL p.n.

Coming Home Hollowing: Pagawewewetung; 1837 t.s. Ojibway notable.

Coming Thunder: Wakanjakoga, or Wawkonchawkoohaw; aka Winnoshik, or Winneshiek (the Younger); 1855 t.s.; 1812-1872. Winnebago notable.

Coming Voice: Peetwaweetam; 1837 t.s. Ojibway notable.

Commissioner: Pasequamjis; 1837 t.s. Ojibway notable.

Conner, Henry; aka Wabishkindib; 1837 t.s. Ojibway notable.

Conoy: from Guneu: Long. PA p.n.

Constance Lake: First Nation of Ontario

Continuous Water, or Along the Water's Edge: Animibeegoong; aka Nipigon: So Long that You Cannot See the End of It. ON p.n.

Cook, Louis: aka Atiatoharongwen: His Body Is Taken Down from Hanging, or One Who Pulls Down the People; c1740-1814. Mohawk notable.

Cool Water, or Pure Water: Sandusky. WI p.n.

Copper Thunderbird: aka Norval Morrisseau; Ojibway artist; 1932-2007.

Copway, George; aka Kahgegagahbowh: Stands Fast, Firm Standing, or He Who Stands Forever; Mississauga Ojibway Methodist minister, writer; 1818-1869.

Cord (or Sinew): Hotsinonhyahta; aka Bunt; fl. 1748-1774. Onondaga notable.

Coshocton: Union of Waters, or Black Bear Town. OH p.n.

Couchiching: At the Edge of a Whirlpool, or Narrows Separating Two Lakes, or Group of Pine Trees. Ontario First Nation.

Cougar (or Panther) Place: Erie; or (less likely) from Yenrash: It Is Long-tailed, or Panther. PA p.n.

Crane (Cry of the): Miami. from Meahme (or Wemiamik): All Friends; aka the Pahkah Miami: or from Omaumeg: People who Live on the Peninsula; or Beautiful Miami; self-desig. Twightwee, or Twatwa: Cry of the Crane. Indiana tribe (not state or federally recognized).

Crane: Chejauk; fl. 1761-1804. Ojibway/Ottawa notable.

Crane: Peytshunkaw; 1829 t.s. Winnebago notable.

Cree: from the French, Kristinaux (ntg); self-desig. Iyiniwok: Those of the First Race. Ontario Tribe/First Nation.

Creek with Pool: Pekstank; source of Paxton Creek. PA p.n.

Crooked Arm: Kawwashkenekay; 1863 t.s. Ojibway notable.

Crooked River: Cuyahoga, or Important River, or Lake River. OH p.n.

Crooked River: Manistee (and Manistique); or Red River, or Wind Sound, or Lost River, or Wood's Spirit. MI p.n.

Crooked Tail: Maunkkayraykau; 1829 t.s. Winnebago notable.

Crooked Way (or Where the River Turns); from Wawiyatanong. Original name for Detroit. Also possibly from Yondotiga: Great Village; or Karontaen: Coast of the Straits. MI p.n.

Cross a Point: Keweenaw. or Portage. MI p.n.

Crossing Sky: Ahahjawwakeshick, or Iaweshowekeshig; 1854, 1855, 1863 t.s. Ojibway notable.

Crouching Lynx: Tukaubishoo; 1825 t.s. Ojibway notable.

Crow Feather: Cawcangewegwan; 1855 t.s. Ojibway notable.

Crow Killer: Kaurahkawseekan; 1829 t.s. Winnebago notable.

Crow Wing: from Kagiwigwan: Crow (or Raven's) Wing, or Raven Feather. MN p.n.

Crow: Enewame; 1815 t.s. Ojibway notable.

Crow: Kankakee: IL p.n

Crow-nesting Place, or Fishing Place, or Long Portage; Okakaning: source of Kaukauna. WI p.n.

Cry of the Crane: Miami. from Meahme (or Wemiamik): All Friends; aka the Pahkah Miami: or from Omaumeg: People who Live on the Peninsula; or Beautiful Miami; self-desig. Twightwee, or Twatwa: Cry of the Crane. Indiana tribe (not state or federally recognized).

Curling Hair: Babaseekundade; 1825 t.s. Ojibway notable.

Curve Lake; First Nation of Ontario

Cusick, Albert: aka Sagonehguahdeh: Provoker; 19th c. Onondaga notable.

Cut Ear: Kisketawak; 1837 t.s. Ojibway notable.

Cut Tails, or Bear Clan: Kiskakon; Nassauaketon: People of the Fork; Sable: Sandy Country People; Sinago: Squirrel Clan. Ottawa divisions.

Cuyahoga: Important River, Crooked, or Lake River. OH p.n.

- *D* -

Dahguoadah (ntg); aka Noah Silversmith; 1838 t.s. Onondaga notable.

d'Aigle, Michel: aka Migisi: Eagle; aka Dokis; c1818-1906; 1854, 1855 t.s.; Ontario First Nation. Ojibway notable.

Dakota: Friend, or Ally; Tribal name, MN p.n.

Dandy: Ogemaga; 1837 t.s. Ojibway notable.

Dark-colored Water (or Shallow Bed River):Tahquamenon. MI p.n.

Daughter: Winona, First-Born Daughter. IN p.n., MI p.n.

Davis, Thomas: aka Tehowagherengaraghkwen (ntg); c1755-c1840. Mohawk notable.

Dead Trees Country: Mishawaka: from M'sehwahkeeki: Country of Dead Trees. IN p.n.

Deaf Thunder: Waukauntshaneekau; 1829 t.s. Winnebago notable.

Decora, Little; aka Mawhecooshawnawzhekaw: One that Stands And Reaches the Sky; 1797-1887; 1855 t.s. Winnebago notable.

Decora, Spoon; aka Choukeka: The Ladle; c1730-1816. Winnebago notable.

Decora, Waukon; aka Waukonhawkaw: White Eagle; ?-c1859. Winnebago notable.

Deep Dry Water Place (dry in summer): Temiscaming. ON p.n.

Deep Water by the Shore: Temagami First Nation (Ontario)

Deep Water, or In the Deep Water: Timiskaming. ON p.n.

Deep Water: Timagami. ON p.n.

Deer House: from Tieranensanoken; aka Peter Herring, 19th c. Turtle clan leader. Mohawk notable.

Deer Lake: First Nation of Ontario

Deer: Scioto; OH, WV p.n.

Deer: Skenandoa; 1706-1816. Oneida notable.

Degonwadonti: She Who is Outnumbered, or Several Against One; aka Brant, Beth; writer, poet; 1941-2015. Mohawk notable.

Dejop: Four Lakes; original name for Madison. WI p.n.

Dekanawida: Two Rivers Flowing Together; Iroquois prophet and co-founder (with Hiawatha) of the League of the Iroquois; 1550?-1600? Iroquois notable.

Delaware River; was originally called Lenape Wihittuck: River of the Lenape, or Maksrick-kitton: Large River. PA p.n.

Delaware subgroup; aka Stockbridge-Munsee; an amalgamated tribe of Stockbridge people made up of Mahican and other, and the Munsee who were moved by the government to Wisconsin from the northeast in the 1840s. WI tribe.

Delaware; First Nation of Ontario

Delight of Life: Leelanau County given "Indian-sounding" name by Indian Agent Henry Rowe Schoolcraft, possibly meant to refer to Delight of Life. There is no "L" sound in the Ojibway language. MI p.n.

Deondo: Trees Growing Out of the Water: possible source of Toronto: Fallen Trees in the Water, or Meeting Place; or from Kanitareonto: Bay in the Lake, or Opening; or from Thorontohen: Timbers on the Water. ON p.n.

Destroyer of Towns: George Washington. The Iroquois called George Washington, Honandaganius: Destroyer of Towns (since then, applied to US Presidents generally).

Detroit River; aka Wahweahtunong (see next). IN, MI p.n.

Detroit; orig. Wawiyatanong: Where the River Turns, or Crooked Way; Yondotiga: Great Village; or Karontaen: Coast of the Straits. MI p.n.

Devil Standing: Menitugawboway, or Mintougaboit; 1815, 1817 t.s. Ottawa notable.

Devil's Bird: Manitobinince; 1868 t.s. (CDN-18). Ojibway notable.

Deyotha'gwende: Through the Opening, or Open Voice; aka Gawehe (ntg); ?-1766. Oneida notable.

Dietz, Angel DeCora; aka Hinookmahiwi-Kilinaka: Fleecy Cloud Floating Into Place, or Woman Coming on the Clouds in Glory; artist, writer, activist; c1871-1919. Winnebago notable.

Diggings of Yellow Plant Root (Moonseed): from Pezhihutazizi Kapi: Yellow Medicine. MN p.n.

Disappearing River, Needle, Awl, Noise Underground, Reed-Like, Thundering Under the Ground, or Something that Pierces: Sheboygan; or from Shabwawagoning: Rumbling Waters, or Waters Disappearing Underground. WI p.n.

Disciple: Meshenawway; 1854 t.s. Ojibway notable.

Diver: Kokomo: Black Walnut, or The Diver. IN p.n.

Dog: Tondawganie (Toutogana, Tontegenah, or Tontagimi); 1805, 1815, 1817, 1818 t.s. Ottawa notable.

Dog; Prairie du Chien; named after Fox chief known as Dog. WI p.n.

Dog's Head: Chonquepa; 1825 t.s. Winnebago notable.

Dokis: aka Migisi: Eagle; aka Michel d'Aigle; c1818-1906; 1854, 1855 t.s.; Ontario First Nation. Ojibway notable.

Door County; orig. Kenatao: Cape. WI p.n.

Door Peninsula; Miami: (The Door) Peninsula Dwellers. WI tribe.

Double Life: from Jeyunghehkwung: aka Johnson, George H. M.; aka Onwanonsyshon (ntg); Six Nations chief; 1816-1884. Mohawk notable.

Double Stream: Neshannock. PA p.n.

Double Wampum: from Tekahionwake: aka Johnson, Emily Pauline; writer, poet; 1861-1913. Mohawk notable.

Dowagiac: Subsistance Area. MI p.n.

Dressing Bird: Naynawonggaybe; 1854 t.s. Ojibway notable.

Dried-up Stream: Iskapiciwan; aka Grassy Narrows. ON p.n.

Drifted Snow: Chanlyeya; aka Joseph Snow; 19th c. Onondaga notable.

Driving Clouds: Natgeeshig; 1836 t.s. Ojibway notable.

Dropping Wind: Mayshueeyaush, or Mayzhakeosh; 1863, 1864 t.s. Ojibway notable.

Duck Feather: Zheewegonab; fl. 1780-1805. Ojibway notable.

Duck: Wheankkaw; 1828 t.s. Winnebago notable.

Dwellers on the Other Side: Outagamie. WI p.n.

Dwelling At Knife Lake: Isanti. MN p.n.

- *E* -

Each Side of the Day: Adawegeshik (or Adawwegezhick), or Both Ends of the Sky. 1837, 1854 t.s. Ojibway notable.

Eagle Head: Horahpawkaw; 1832 t.s. Winnebago notable.

Eagle Lake: First Nation of Ontario

Eagle, Red War: Heetshahwaushaipsootskau; 1829 t.s. Winnebago notable.

Eagle, War: Horahoankkaw; 1832 t.s. Winnebago notable.

Eagle, White War: Heetshawausharpskawkau; 1829, 1832 t.s. Winnebago notable.

Eagle: Peneshaw; 1818 t.s. Ottawa notable.

Earth Paint Pigment: Mankato: or Blue Earth, (site of largest mass execution in U.S. history, where 38 Dakota were hanged on Dec. 26, 1862; see list on p.42) . MN p.n.

Earth: Maunkawkaw; 1829 t.s. Winnebago notable.

Eau Claire: French for Clear Water: from Wayaconuttaquayaw Sebe: Water (of the River) Is Clear. WI p.n.

Eddy: Kawachewan; 1805 t.s. Ottawa notable.

Edge of a Whirlpool: Couchiching. ON p.n.

Eel Place: Shamokin. PA p.n.

Eel: Shakanak: Slippery Fish (eel). IN p.n.

Eeneewonkshikkaw: Stone Man; 1832 t.s. Winnebago notable.

Eezhookhattaykaw: Big Gun; 1832 t.s. Winnebago notable.

Elder Brother: K-che-osauya; 1837 t.s. Ojibway notable.

Elder Brother's Son: Capemabe; 1847 t.s. Ojibway notable.

Elk: Mushkoas; 1825 t.s. Ojibway notable.

Elkhart: from Mesheh-wehoudehik: Elk Heart (from an island of this shape). IN p.n.

End of the Lake: Wanikamiu; aka Fond du Lac. WI p.n.

Enemy: Modoc: from Shasteeca word for Enemy. IN p.n.

Enewame: Crow; 1815 t.s. Ojibway notable.

Enlightener: Onkhiswathetani; aka Swateny; aka Ongwaterohiathe: He Lightens the Sky for Us; ?-1748. Oneida notable.

Enneasnekauntaa: Small Stick of Wood; aka White, Angus; 19th c. Snipe Clan leader. Mohawk notable.

Equal Sky: Tebishcogeshick; 1864 t.s. Ojibway notable.

Erdrich, Louise; aka Kino-gune-beek (ntg); writer, poet; 1954- Ojibway notable.

Erie: from the Iroquoian, Erielhonan: Long Tail (a reference to the cougar or mountain lion), or Panther. Ohio tribe. NY, OH, ON, PA p.n.

Escanaba: Flat Rock. MI p.n.

Eshkebugecoshe: Flat Mouth; Leech Lake Ojibway; 1774-1860. Ojibway notable.

Eshtonoquot: Clear Sky; aka Francis McCoonse; 1836, 1859 t.s. Ojibway notable.

Etobicoke: from Wahdobekaung; Forest of Alders, or Place Where Alders Grow. ON p.n.

Everlasting Sky: Kaugaygeezhig; 1837 t.s. Ojibway notable.

Expert Boy: Acqueweezais, or Wickedly Expert; 1837 t.s. Ojibway notable.

Extensive Flats: M'chevomi; source of Wyoming. PA p.n.

- ℱ -

Fair to Look Upon: Ohio, or Beautiful River, or Large River, or simply Beautiful; other sources claim that the word is only a prefix meaning White Caps (or simply White). The full word for the river should then be Ohio-pek-hanne: River Whitened By Froth; or Ohiophanne: River Full of White Caps, or Very White River; also a CO, IL, IN, KY, NY, PA, WV place name.

Fair, Fertile Land: Mino-aki; aka Milwaukee; or from Mene-awkee; Good Earth, or Rich Land. WI p.n.

Falcon: Shawshawwanebase; aka John Tanner; adopted, lived as Ojibway, narrated biography; c1780-1846? Ojibway notable.

Fallen Trees in the Water, or Meeting Place: Toronto; or from Deondo: Trees Growing Out of the Water; or from Kanitareonto: Bay in the Lake, or Opening; or from Thorontohen: Timbers on the Water. ON p.n.

Far Away Land: Wausaukee. WI p.n.

Far Away: Wausau. WI p.n.

Far Off: Washtenaw; or On the River. MI p.n.

Farmer, Orris; aka Hodegweh: Absconder; 19th c. Onondaga notable.

Farthest Point of the Lake: from Wanikamiu: Fond du Lac: or End of the Lake; French adaptation. Minnesota reservation.

Feather in the Meadow: Mushkootagwima, or Meadow Sparrow; 1837 t.s. Ojibway notable.

Feather: Naquanabie; 1837 t.s. Ojibway notable.

Feeding Place of Bears: Macungy. PA p.n.

Fiddler, Jack; aka Zhuawuno-geezhigo-gaubow: He Who Stands in the Southern Sky; aka Maisaninnine: Stylish Person; c1830-1907. Ojibway notable.

Fierce Heart: Nathkaysawkaw; 1828 t.s. Winnebago notable.

Figure Carved on a Tree: Venango. PA p.n.

Fine Day: Hompskakah; 1837 t.s. Winnebago notable.

Fine Day: Menogeshick; 1863 t.s. Ojibway notable.

Fire Holder: Pashkayraykaw; 1832 t.s. Winnebago notable.

Fire Nation: Potawatomi. or People of the Place of the Fire, or Keepers of the Sacred Fire; responsible for the Three Fires Confederacy council fire; self-desig. Anishnabek: Original People, or Those Who Intend To Do Well. Michigan Tribe.

Firm Standing: from Kahgegagahbowh; or He Who Stands Forever: aka George Copway; writer and Methodist minister; 1818-1869. Mississauga notable.

First Actor: Kelystum; 1815 t.s. Ottawa notable.

First Day: Wenghegesheguk; 1837 t.s. Ojibway notable.

First Sky: Nawtawmegezhick; 1854 t.s. Ojibway notable.

First to Start the Whites: Wassachum; 1815 t.s. Ottawa notable.

First-Born Daughter: Winona. IN, MI, MN p.n.

First-Born Son: Chaska. MN p.n.

Fish (sturgeon or catfish): Merrimac. WI p.n.

Fish Bait Place: Watonwan; or Where Fish Abound. MN p.n.

Fish Eaters, or People of the Sea; possible meanings of Winnebago; said to be from a Potawatomi word, Winpyeko, which means People of the Dirty Water, in reference to Green Bay, Wisconsin, their traditional homeland; self-designations said to be Hochunkgra: People of the Big Voice, Hutcangara: Big Fish People, or Hochagra: People of the Parent Speech; the Wisconsin tribe has officially changed its name to Ho-chunk Nation: People of the First Voice; Nebraska, Wisconsin tribe; IL, MN, NE, WI p.n.

Fish Fence at the Narrows: Chippewas of Mnjikaning; aka Rama First Nation (Ontario)

Fish Leap Over the Water: Gogama. ON p.n.

Fish Spearing Place: Algonkin. Ontario Tribe/First Nation.

Fishing Place, or Crow-nesting Place, or Long Portage: Okakaning; source of Kaukauna. WI p.n.

Flame: Nangotuck; 1825 t.s. Ojibway notable.

Flat Land: Pays Plat (French); former name for Baagwaashiing First Nation (Ontario): Where the Water is Shallow

Flat Mouth: Aishkebogekoshe, or Eshkebugecoshe; 1837, 1847, 1855 t.s.; 1774-1860; Leech Lake Ojibway notable.

Flat Rock: Escanaba. MI p.n.

Fleecy Cloud Floating Into Place, or Woman Coming on the Clouds in Glory: Hinook-ma-hiwi-Kilinaka; aka Angel DeCora Dietz; artist, writer, activist; c1871-1919. Winnebago notable.

Flint (several variations); MOHAWK - most often translated as Man-eaters, or Cannibals; possibly from Mohowauuck: They Eat Animate Things; also translated as Keepers of the Eastern Door. several self-designations; Ongwe-howe: Real People, Cannieigas: Flint People, Kanien'kéhaka: People of the Flint, and Gäneagaono: Possessors of the Flint; New York, Ontario, Quebec tribe (the Akwesasne Mohawk are of New York); part of the Iroquois confederacy; all of Mohawk territory is called Kanienkeh: Land of the Flint.

Flintstone: Peawanuck; new name for Winisk. ON p.n.

Floating Bridge: Owasco. IN p.n.

Flour: Napanee. ON p.n.

Flowing Out (as a river into a lake): Oswego. WI p.n.

Flying Around: Kewetayash; (one Canadian treaty [CDN-124], signed in 1871, listed the signers as "Ojibway/Cree").

Flying Cloud: Mauheeherkarrah; 1832 t.s. Winnebago notable.

Flying Down Bird: Nashake; (one Canadian treaty [CDN-124], signed in 1871, listed the signers as "Ojibway/Cree").

Flying Post: First Nation of Ontario

Fond du Lac: End of the Lake; French adaptation of Wanikamiu: Farthest Point of the Lake; End of the Lake. Minnesota reservation.

Foremost Sitter: Nawgawnub; 1854 t.s. Ojibway notable.

Forest of Alders: Wahdobekaung; Etobicoke; or Place Where Alders Grow. ON p.n.

Forked River: Nissowaquet; c1715-1797. Ottawa notable.

Forked Tail: Weetshahunkuk; 1832 t.s. Winnebago notable.

Forks of the Stream: Lechauhannek; source of Lackawanna. PA p.n.

Fort Albany: First Nation of Ontario

Fort Severn: First Nation of Ontario

Fort William: First Nation of Ontario

Forward Man: Naugaunosh;1825 t.s. Ojibway notable.

Four Fingers: Neoning; 1866 t.s. Ojibway notable.

Four Lakes: Dejop; original name for Madison. WI p.n.

Four Legs: Hootshoapkau; 1828, 1829, 1832 t.s. Winnebago notable.

Four Skies: Neokeshick; 1863 t.s. Ojibway notable.

Four Who Stand: Thoapnuzheekaw; 1829 t.s. Winnebago notable.

Foxes, or Big Fox, or Good Land River; Waushara. WI p.n.

Foxes: Wakusheg; source of Waukesha. WI p.n.

Friends: Miami. from Meahme (or Wemiamik): All Friends; aka the Pahkah Miami: or from Omaumeg: People who Live on the Peninsula; or Beautiful Miami; self-desig. Twightwee, or Twatwa: Cry of the Crane. Indiana tribe:

Funnel: Cheboygan (or Pipe. or from Shabwawagoning: Rumbling Waters, or Waters Disappearing Underground. MI p.n.

Furious Dog: Tondagonee; 1837 t.s. Ojibway notable.

- *G* -

Gabeshcodaway: Going Through the Prairie; 1866 t.s. Ojibway notable.

Gahaehdaseah: Whirlwind; aka Abram Hill; 19th c. Oneida notable.

Gamanautigawaeyauk: Land of Many River Islands; original name for Thunder Bay: Animikie Wekwed. ON p.n.

Gananoque: Rocks in Deep Water, or Rocks Rising Out of River. ON p.n.

Ganawawbamina: He Who Is Looked At; 1866 t.s. Ojibway notable.

Gäneagaono (Possessors of the Flint): Mohawk. or Kaniekahaka (People of the Flint).

Ganshowehanne: Roaring Stream, or Noisy Stream Flowing Over; original name for Schuylkill: Hidden River (perhaps a Dutch word and not Native at all). PA p.n.

Garakonthie: Moving Sun; aka Daniel peace leader; 1600-1676. Onondaga notable.

Garden River: from Kitiganisibi. Ontario First Nation.

Garlic: Chicago; possibly from Chicacwa: Garlic, Onion, Leek, Onion Place, or Garlic Field. IL, WI p.n.

Garonhiague: Celestial, or In the Sky; aka Ogenheratarihiens: Hot Ash; aka; c1646-1687. Mohawk notable.

Gasagaskwajimekang: Leech Lake; There Are Leeches There, or Full of Leeches. MN p.n.

Gate, or Place Between Two Points, or Peaceful Valley, or Place of Entrance (or The Gate), or At the Forks: Tioga. PA p.n.

Gathering of the Waters: Weeskonsan; possible source of Wisconsin : possible meanings: Muskrat Land, Grassy Place; or from Meskousing: Where the Waters Gather, Place of the Red Earth People, or Red Stone; or from Misconsin: Strong Current.

Gawababiganikag: the White Earth Reservation; aka White Clay, or Gawababigunikag Sagaiigun: White Clay Place. MN p.n.

Gawnandawawinzo: Berry Hunter; 1866 t.s. Ojibway notable.

Geauga: Racoon. OH p.n.

General, Alexander; aka Deskahe (ntg); Cayuga/Oneida; 1889-1965.

Genesee, from Gennesheyo: Beautiful Valley. IN, MI, PA, WI p.n.

George Copway; aka Kahgegagahbowh: He Who Stands Forever, or Firm Standing; writer and Methodist minister; 1818-1869. Mississauga notable.

George Kachenooting (ntg); Henry Bird Steinhauer; aka Sowengisik (ntg); Ojibway educator; c1818-1884. Ojibway notable.

George Washington. The Iroquois called George Washington, Honandaganius: Destroyer of Towns (since then, applied to US Presidents generally).

George, Daniel; aka Johahgoehdeh: Road Scraper; 19th c. Onondaga notable

George, George; aka Skahlohahdieh: Beyond the Sky; 19th c. Oneida notable.

George, Solomon; aka Walhahleigh: Watchful; 19th c. Oneida notable.

Giant: Mesabi (or Missabi); or Hidden Giant (Iron Range name). MN, WI p.n.

Ginoogaming (formerly known as Long Lake 77 First Nation); First Nation of Ontario

Ginozhaekaunning: Pike Place. Original name for Bay Mills Indian Community. Michigan reservation.

Glikhikan: Gun Sight; aka Isaac; Munsee/Delaware; c1730-1782 (killed at Gnadenhutten massacre). Munsee notable.

Gnat Place, or Sand-fly Town: Punxsutawney. PA p.n.

God Almighty: Shamanetoo; 1815 t.s. Ojibway notable.

Gogama: Fish Leap Over the Water. ON p.n.

Gogebic: Green Lake, High Lake, On the Rock, or Trembling Ground. MI, WI p.n.

Going Home, or Going Back: Keewaywin First Nation (Ontario)

Going Through the Prairie: Gabeshcodaway; 1866 t.s. Ojibway notable.

Golden Eagle: Kineubenae; Mississauga; fl. 1797-1812 Ojibway notable.

Good Earth, or Rich Land: Mene-awkee; aka Milwaukee; or from Mino-aki: Fair, Fertile Land. WI p.n.

Good Heart: Nautshkaypeenkaw; 1832 t.s. Winnebago notable.

Good Land River, Big Fox, or Foxes: Waushara. WI p.n.

Good Potato Place: Topeka (from the Shawnee word for Jerusalem Artichoke). IN p.n.

Good Thunder: Wakuntchapinka; c1790-1863. Winnebago notable.

Goods Brought In: Potomac: Where Goods Are Brought In. IL p.n.

Goose: Weetshunkaw; 1832 t.s. Winnebago notable.

Grand Blanc: aka Sawanabenase: Southern Bird; aka Pechegabua; 1807 t.s. Ojibway notable.

Grand Canoe: Watchkatoque; 1825 t.s. Winnebago notable.

Grand Marais; orig. Kitchi-bitobigong: Great Pond Place. MI, MN p.n.

Grand Portage: Kitchi-Winigumeeng. MN p.n.

Grand River Band of Ottawa Indians: State-recognized Tribe of Michigan.

Grand Sable Dunes; orig. Nigowidjiw: Sand Mountain. MI p.n.

Granite People: from Onayotekäono; the Oneida, or from Onuyo'teaka': People of the Standing (or Upright) Stone, or Stone People; aka Ratirontakowa: People of the Big Log; New York, Ontario, Wisconsin tribe; part of the Iroquois Conf.; NY, TN, WI p.n.

Grassy Narrows: aka Asubpeeschoseewagong (ntg); First Nation of Ontario

Grassy Narrows; aka Iskapiciwan: Dried-up Stream. ON p.n.

Grassy Place, or Muskrat Land; possible meanings of Wisconsin ; or from Meskousing: Where the Waters Gather, Place of the Red Earth People, or Red Stone; or from Misconsin: Strong Current; or from Weeskonsan: Gathering of the Waters.

Grassy River Mouth: Madawaska. ON p.n.

Gray Slate Bay: Sheguiandah First Nation (Ontario)

Great (or Big) Cloud: Cheonoquet (or Cheanaquod); 1825, 1837 t.s. Ojibway notable.

Great Bend River: Guneshachachgak-hanne; possible source of Susquehanna: Muddy River. PA p.n.

Great Falls: Kitchi-Gaugeedjiwunng; aka Niagara: Bisected Bottom Lands, Neck of Land Between Lakes, Thunder of Waters, or Resounding with Great Noise. ON p.n.

Great Hill People: Nundawaono; or Tsionontowanehaka (People of the Big Mountain); self. desig. of the Seneca. Ontario Tribe/First Nation.

Great Lake (of the Ojibway): Kitchi-gummeng. Original name for Lake Superior. MI p.n.

Great Lake; possible meaning of Ontario; or from Kanadario: Sparkling Water; or from Onitariio: Beautiful Lake; or from Ontarack: Rocks Standing High in the Water; other possible meanings:, Beautiful Lake, Handsome Lake, or Large Lake; NY, OR, WI p.n.

Great Law. Iroquois Confederacy: There is much evidence to suggest that the Iroquois Confederacy's founding document, The Great Law (Gayaneshagowa), was used as the framework for the U.S. Constitution by the Founding Fathers.

Great Medicine People: the Ojibway, or Chippewa. See p. 99 for complete discussion.

Great Noise: Sheboygan. ON p.n.

Great Pond Place: Grand Marais; orig. Kitchi-bitobigong. MN p.n.

Great Turtle (Place of), or Large Turtle Island: from Michilimackinak: Mackinac (also spelled, and pronounced, Mackinaw). MI p.n.

Great Village: Yondotiga. Original name for Detroit. Also, Wawiyatanong: Where the River Turns, or Crooked Way; or Karontaen: Coast of the Straits. MI p.n.

Green Bay; orig. Pujikut: Bay in Spite of Everything. WI p.n.

Green Lake, or On the Rock: Gogebic. MI, WI p.n.

Gross Guelle: aka Kweeweezaishish (ntg); 1825 t.s. Ojibway notable.

Group of Pine Trees, At the Edge of a Whirlpool, or Narrows Separating Two Lakes: Couchiching. Ontario First Nation.

Gull Bay: First Nation of Ontario

Gun Lake Tribe: now known as Match-e-be-nash-she-wish Band of Pottawatomi Indians: Bad Bird; Michigan Reservation

Gun Sight: from Glikhikan; aka Isaac; Munsee/Delaware; c1730-1782 (killed at Gnadenhutten massacre). Munsee notable.

Guneshachachgak-hanne: Great Bend River; possible source of Susquehanna: Muddy River. PA p.n.

Guneu: Long; source of Conoy. PA p.n.

Gwartheelass: He Leads the People; aka Leonard Peltier; Ojibway-Lakota activist, political prisoner; 1944- Ojibway notable.

Gweugwehono (People at the Mucky Land): Cayuga. or Siotinonawentowane (People of the Big Pipe).

- *H* -

Hackmatack: Bad Lowlands (that is, the place where these trees grow); source of Tamarack. PA p.n.

Hakahkah: Little Boy Child; 1837 t.s. Winnebago notable.

Haksigaxunuminka: Little Fish Daughter; aka Kehachiwinga: Wolf's Mountain Home Maker; aka Mountain Wolf Woman; writer; 1884-1960. Winnebago notable.

Halfday: Aptakisic. IL p.n.

Half-way Water: Abitibi (in reference to trading posts in either direction). ON p.n.

Hammelin, Augustin Jr.; aka Kanapima: One Who Is Talked About; 1813-?. Ottawa notable.

Handsome Lake; possible meaning of Ontario; or from Kanadario: Sparkling Water; or from Onitariio: Beautiful Lake; or from Ontarack: Rocks Standing High in the Water; other possible meanings: Great Lake, Beautiful Lake, or Large Lake; NY, OR, WI p.n.

Hat-rim Protects the Neck: from Ta-ra-ke-te; aka Tarbell, Philip; 19th c. Wolf clan Mohawk chief. Mohawk notable.

Haudenosaunee: People of the Longhouse; aka Iroquois: from the Algonquin, Irinakhoiw: Rattlesnakes; Ontario Tribe/First Nation.

Haukkaykaw: Screamer; 1832 t.s. Winnebago notable.

Haunheighkeepawkaw: Night that Meets; 1832 t.s. Winnebago notable.

Haupmeemannekaw: He Who Walks By Day; 1828 t.s. Winnebago notable.

Hayahdugihwah: Bitter Body; aka Thomas Webster; 19th c. keeper of the wampum for the League of the Iroquois. Onondaga notable.

Haynahahratshkay: Left-handed; 1829 t.s. Winnebago notable.

Haynoampkaw: Two Horns; 1832 t.s. Winnebago notable.

Hayouwaesh: Intestine Bruiser; aka Daniel La Forte; 19th c. Chairman of the League of the Iroquois. Onondaga notable.

Hayraytshonsarp: Black Hawk; 1829 t.s. Winnebago notable.

Hayrokawkaw: Without Horns; 1828 t.s. Winnebago notable.

Hazeekaw: Yellow Bank; 1855 t.s. Winnebago notable.

Hazhunkeetaw: One Horn; 1855 t.s. Winnebago notable.

He Causes It to Be Light for Us: Stayeghtha; Oneida notable.

He Has Made the Mist Disappear for Them, or Disappearing Knot: from Sakayengwaraton: aka John Johnson; aka Smoke Johnson; Pinetree chief; 1792-1886. Mohawk notable.

He Has Placed Two Worlds Together: from Tehoragwanegen: aka Thomas Williams; c1758-1849. Mohawk notable.

He is to Blame: from Archsisorihenn; aka Solomon, Alexander;19th c. leader. Mohawk notable.

He Leads the People: Gwartheelass; aka Leonard Peltier; Ojibway-Lakota activist, political prisoner; 1944- Ojibway notable.

He Makes Rivers (from Haio-hwa'tha): Hiawatha. Mohawk co-founder (with Dekanawida) of the League of the Iroquois; 1525?-1575? Iroquois notable.

He Moves About: Kickapoo. WI p.n.

He Places Together Two Bets: from Thayendanegea: aka Joseph Brant.1743?-1807. Mohawk notable.

He that Gathers Berries: Cawwindow; 1825 t.s. Ojibway notable.

He that Is Spoken To: Maydwaguanonind; 1864 t.s. Ojibway notable.

He that Kills the Crow: Caricasica; 1825 t.s. Winnebago notable.

He that Leaves the Yellow Track: Sawwaughkeewau; 1828 t.s. Winnebago notable.

He Walks Ahead (ie. the pioneer): Negaunee. MI p.n.

He Who Comes Shining, or One Who Makes the World Brighter: Pahtahsega: aka Peter Jones; Mississauga Ojibway, Methodist minister; c1807-1890. Ojibway notable.

He Who Inhabits: Abetang. 1866 t.s. Ojibway notable.

He Who Is Looked At: Ganawawbamina: 1866 t.s. Ojibway notable.

He Who Is Master of the Lodge: Wautsherookunahkaw; 1828, 1829 t.s. Winnebago notable.

He Who Plays with the Ox: Tshayoskawtshokaw; 1829 t.s. Winnebago notable.

He Who Sits Quietly: Topinabee. Notable 19th c. Potawatomi chief who signed many treaties. MI p.n.

He Who Stands Forever, or Firm Standing: from Kahgegagahbowh: aka George Copway; writer and Methodist minister; 1818-1869. Mississauga notable.

He Who Stands in the House: Tshuonuzheekau; aka Karraymaunee: Walking Turtle; 1829, 1832 t.s. Winnebago notable.

He Who Stands in the Southern Sky: Zhuawuno-geezhigo-gaubow; aka Maisaninnine: Stylish Person; aka Jack Fiddler; c1830-1907. Ojibway notable.

He Who Takes Up the Snowshoe: Honyere Tehawenkarogwen; Oneida notable.

Heard Fell Down: Matwaash; 1817 t.s. Ojibway notable.

Hearenhodoh: Standing Tree; aka Loft, John; 19th c. leader. Mohawk notable.

Heavy: Le Pesant; aka Bear; fl. 1703-12. Ottawa notable.

Heetshahwaushaipsootskau: Red War Eagle; 1829 t.s. Winnebago notable.

Heetshaumwaukaw: Wild Cat; 1829 t.s. Winnebago notable.

Heetshawausharpskawkau: White War Eagle; 1829, 1832 t.s. Winnebago notable.

Hemp Gatherers, or Shirt Wearing People: Tuscarora. Ontario Tribe/First Nation

Here They Take the Boats Out: Cayuga. ON p.n.

Here We Rest: Weyauwega. WI p.n.

Herring, Peter; aka Tieranensanoken: Deer House; 19th c. Turtle clan leader. Mohawk notable.

Hiawatha (or Haio-hwa'tha): He Makes Rivers; Mohawk co-founder (with Dekanawida) of the League of the Iroquois; 1525?-1575? Mohawk notable. MI p.n.

Hiawatha: First Nation of Ontario

Hidden River: Schuylkill (perhaps a Dutch word and not Native at all); orig. Ganshowehanne: Roaring Stream, or Noisy Stream Flowing Over. PA p.n.

High Lake: Gogebic. or Green Lake, or On the Rock, or Trembling Ground. MI p.n.

High Place: Ishpeming. MI p.n.

High-bush Cranberry River People: Anibiminani Zibi Wininiwug: Pembina; Ojibway band.

Hill (People of): Onondaga: Onundägaono (People of the Hill) or Onontakehaka (People on the Hills)

Hill, Abram; aka Gahaehdaseah: Whirlwind; 19th c. Oneida notable.

Hill, Isaac; aka Teyemthohisa: Two Doors Closed; 19th c. Onondaga notable.

Hill, Norbert S. Jr.; aka Onanquatgo: Big Medicine; educator, author; 1946-. Oneida notable.

Hilly Island, or Bow and Arrow Wood Place: Manhattan. PA p.n.

Hilly Place: Algonquins of Pikwàkanagàn; First Nation of Ontario

Him that Looks Over: Paymaubeemee; 1828 t.s. Winnebago notable.

Hinookmahiwi-Kilinaka: Fleecy Cloud Floating Into Place, or Woman Coming on the Clouds in Glory; aka Angel DeCora Dietz; artist, writer, activist; c1871-1919. Winnebago notable.

His Body Is Taken Down from Hanging, or One Who Pulls Down the People: Atiatoharongwen; aka Louis Cook; c1740-1814. Mohawk notable.

Hoantshskawskaw: White Bear; 1832 t.s. Winnebago notable.

Hochagra: People of the Parent Speech; or Hochunkgra: People of the Big Voice, or Hutcangara: Big Fish People; self-designations of the Winnebago - said to be from a Potawatomi word, Winpyeko, which means People of the Dirty Water, in reference to Green Bay, Wisconsin, their traditional homeland; also said to mean Fish Eaters, or People of the Sea; the Wisconsin tribe has officially changed its name to Ho-chunk Nation: People of the First Voice; Nebraska, Wisconsin tribe; IL, MN, NE, WI p.n.

Ho-chunk Nation: People of the First Voice; the now-officail name of the WINNEBAGO, said to be from a Potawatomi word, Winpyeko, which means People of the Dirty Water, in reference to Green Bay, Wisconsin, their traditional homeland; also said to mean Fish Eaters, or People of the Sea; self-designations said to be Hochunkgra: People of the Big Voice, Hutcangara: Big Fish People, or Hochagra: People of the Parent Speech; the Wisconsin tribe has officially changed its name to; Nebraska, Wisconsin tribe; IL, MN, NE, WI p.n.

Hochunkgra: People of the Big Voice, or Hochagra: People of the Parent Speech; self-designations of the Winnebago - said to be from a Potawatomi word, Winpyeko, which means People of the Dirty Water, in reference to Green Bay, Wisconsin, their traditional homeland; Nebraska, Wisconsin tribe; IL, MN, NE, WI p.n.

Hodegweh: Absconder; Orris Farmer; 19th c. Onondaga notable.

Hodiseññageta: Name Bearers; the ONONDAGA: from Onundägaono: People on (Top of) the Hills, or from Onontakehaka: People of the Hill; New York, Ontario tribe; part of the Iroquois Confederacy; NY p.n.

Hog Place, or Closed in By Fog: Koshkonong. WI p.n.

Hogewayhtah (ntg); aka William Jacket; 1838 t.s. Oneida notable.

Hole in the Day, or Opening in the Sky: from Bugonegijig; 1825-1868. Ojibway notable.

Hole in the Day: Pagoonakeezhig, or Puinanegi; 1825, 1837 t.s. Ojibway notable (father of above).

Hole in the Day: Tugonakeshik;1855 t.s. Ojibway notable.

Hole in the Day: Quewezance (various spellings); 1854, 1855, 1864, 1867 t.s.; also translated as: The Boy; 1864 t.s.; and White Fish; 1854 t.s. Ojibway notable.

Hompskakah: Fine Day; 1837 t.s. Winnebago notable.

Honchhuttakaw: Big Bear; 1855 t.s. Winnebago notable.

Honnonegadoh: Silversmith; 1838 t.s. Oneida notable.

Honyere Tehawenkarogwen: He Who Takes Up the Snowshoe. Oneida notable.

Hoof, Claw, or Nail: Oshkosh; Menominee; 1795-1858. WI p.n.

Hoongkah: Old Chief; 1837 t.s. Winnebago notable.

Hoonkhoonokaw: Little Chief; aka Little Priest; 1855 t.s. Winnebago notable.

Hootshoapkau: Four Legs; 1828, 1829, 1832 t.s. Winnebago notable.

Hoowauneekaw (or Howamicka): Little Elk; 1825, 1828, 1829, 1832 t.s. Winnebago notable.

Hoowayskaw: White Elk; 1832 t.s. Winnebago notable.

Horahoankkaw: War Eagle; 1832 t.s. Winnebago notable.

Horahpawkaw: Eagle Head; 1832 t.s. Winnebago notable.

Horicon: Silver Water. WI p.n.

Hornepayne: First Nation of Ontario

Hot Ash: from Ogenheratarihiens; aka Garonhiague: Celestial, or In the Sky; c1646-1687. Mohawk notable.

Hotsinonhyahta: Cord (or Sinew); aka Bunt; fl. 1748-1774. Onondaga notable.

Howamicka (or Hoowauneekaw): Little Elk; 1825, 1828, 1829, 1832 t.s. Winnebago notable.

Huron (tribal name). OH p.n.

Hutcangara: Big Fish People; or Hochunkgra: People of the Big Voice, or Hochagra: People of the Parent Speech; self-designations of the Winnebago - said to be from a Potawatomi word, Winpyeko, which means People of the Dirty Water, in reference to Green Bay, Wisconsin, their traditional homeland; Nebraska, Wisconsin tribe; IL, MN, NE, WI p.n.

- *I* -

Iaubensee: Little Buck; 1825 t.s. Ojibway notable.

Iaweshowekeshig: Crossing Sky; 1854, 1855 t.s. Ojibway notable.

Iingegaunabe: Wants Feathers; 1864 t.s. Ojibway notable.

ILLINOIS - from Illini: Man; plural, Illiniwok: People, or Perfect and Accomplished Men; Illinois divisions: Cahokia (ntg), and Tamaroa: He Has a Cut Tail; Oklahoma tribe.

Important River: Cuyahoga, or Crooked River, or Lake River. OH p.n.

In a Little Water, At the Place of the Waters or, In the Leaves: Nipissing (Lake); or from Nipisisinan: Little Body of Water (ie. the smallest of the Great Lakes). ON p.n.

In the Leaves, At the Place of the Waters; or In a Little Water: Nipissing (Lake); or from Nipisisinan: Little Body of Water (ie. the smallest of the Great Lakes) . ON p.n.

INDIAN - The use of "Indian" as a collective term for the indigenous people of North America is not generally supported by tribal people. The term is an obvious misnomer applied by Columbus who believed he was in "the Indies." In the 15th c. world of Columbus, any place east of the Indus River (which runs through what is now Pakistan) was "the Indies." Consequently, people who lived in "the Indies" were "Indians." So, in the most generous sense, the word had limited validity; it is true that the people of the "New World" did indeed live "east" of the Indus River. There are some who maintain that "Indian" derives from the Spanish "in dios," a phrase which (it is said) makes a vague reference to the possibility that Columbus viewed Native people as having been created "*in* the image of *God.*" No credible evidence to support the "in dios" source theory can be found; it appears to be of purely romantic origin. As for an appropriate collective term, the author asked tribes in both the U.S. and Canada to offer their suggestions. Those terms with the least support (less than 5%) are: Amerindians (0%), First Americans (1%), First People (1%), American Indians (1%), and Indians (4%). Aboriginal People (6%) and First Nations (11%) fall into a second tier of acceptable alternatives. (First Nations is an "official" Canadian designation, but its support was split almost equally between Canadian and U.S. tribes). Indigenous People (19%) and Native People (22%) were clearly quite acceptable to those responding, but the most acceptable alternative to Indian is "Native American" which received support from one-third of all respondents. What term to use? In Canada, no one will raise an eyebrow over Aboriginal People and/or First Nations (which seems to be gaining in popularity), and everywhere, Indigenous People, Native People, and Native Americans seem to be quite acceptable as well.

INDIANA - obvious source of its name is from its indigenous inhabitants

Indiana tribe: Miami, from Omaumeg: People who Live on the Peninsula; or from Meahme (or Wemiamik): All Friends; aka the Pahkah Miami: Beautiful Miami; self-desig. Twightwee, or Twatwa: Cry of the Crane.

Intestine Bruiser: Hayouwaesh; aka Daniel La Forte; 19th c. Chairman of the League of the Iroquois. Onondaga notable.

Irinakhoiw (possibly from the Algonquin): IROQUOIS - meaning Rattlesnakes, or Real Adders.

Iron: Pewabik. WI p.n.

IROQUOIS - possibly from the Algonquin, Irinakhoiw, meaning Rattlesnakes, or Real Adders; also it is claimed that it is a French rendition of a Basque word reportedly meaning, The Killer People; self-desig. Haudenosaunee: People of the Longhouse; the equivalent word in Mohawk is Onkwehonwe, which means The Real People, or People Surpassing All Others; the Iroquois can be found in New York, Ontario, Oklahoma, Quebec, and Wisconsin.

Iroquois Confederacy: There is much evidence to suggest that the Iroquois Confederacy's founding document, The Great Law (Gayaneshagowa), was used as the framework for the U.S. Constitution by the Founding Fathers. The Iroquois called George Washington, Honandaganius: Destroyer of Towns (since then, applied to US Presidents generally). Members of the Iroquois Confederacy (from east to west) are: Seneca, Cayuga, Onondaga, Oneida, Mohawk.

Iroquois: Real Adders. ON p.n.

Iroquois; Irinakhoiw: Rattlesnakes (from the Algonquin); self-desig. Haudenosaunee: People of the Longhouse. Ontario Tribe/First Nation.

Isaac; aka Glikhikan: Gun Sight; Munsee/Delaware; c1730-1782 (killed at Gnadenhutten massacre). Munsee notable.

Isanti: Dwelling At Knife Lake. MN p.n.

Ishpeming: High Place. MI p.n.

Ishtakhaba: Sleepy Eyes; after the Sisseton Dakota leader of the late 1800s. MN p.n.

Iskapiciwan: Dried-up Stream; aka Grassy Narrows. ON p.n.

Iskutewizaagegan: (ntg) (Formerly known as Shoal Lake 39 First Nation of Ontario)

Island in the Lake: Munising. MI p.n.

Island of the Spirit, or Great Spirit Cave: Manitoulin; or a corruption of Manitowaning: At the Spirit's Cave (the root, Manitou, means Spirit). ON p.n.

Islanders: Wyandotte, or Peninsula Dwellers. MI, OH p.n.

It Is Mixed: Kinnickinnic (a smoking mixture of tobacco, sumac, and red willow). WI p.n.

Iyawbance: Little Buck; 1854 t.s. Ojibway notable.

Iyiniwok: Those of the First Race; aka Cree; Cree is from the French, Kristinaux (ntg). Ontario Tribe/First Nation.

- J -

Jacket, William; aka Hogewayhtah (ntg); 1838 t.s. Oneida notable.

Jahdahdieh: Sailing Whale; aka Jaris Pierce; 19th c. clerk of the Six Nations. Onondaga notable.

Jaybird: Pensweguesic; 1817 t.s. Ojibway notable.

Jeyunghehkwung: Double Life; aka Johnson, George H. M.; aka Onwanonsyshon (ntg); Six Nations chief; 1816-1884. Mohawk notable.

Jikagons: Chicago: possibly from Jikagons: Skunk, Polecat Place, or Kitten Skunk Place. IL p.n.

Johahgoehdeh: Road Scraper; aka Daniel George; 19th c. Onondaga notable.

John, William; aka Kanohquasa (ntg); 1838 t.s. Onondaga notable.

Johnson, Emily Pauline; aka Tekahionwake: Double Wampum; writer, poet; 1861-1913. Mohawk notable.

Johnson, George Henry Martin; aka Jeyunghehkwung: Double Life; aka Onwanonsyshon (ntg); Six Nations chief; 1816-1884. Mohawk notable.

Johnson (or Johnston), John; aka Sakayengwaraton: He Has Made the Mist Disappear for Them, or Disappearing Knot; aka Smoke Johnson; Pinetree chief; 1792-1886. Mohawk notable.

Johnston, William; aka Tekawironte: Two Infants Stand Out; c1750-1777. Mohawk notable.

Jones, Joshua; aka Sasunnahgandeeh: Half Name, or Half Blood; 19th c. Oneida notable.

Jones, Peter; aka Kahkewaquonaby: Sacred Feathers; Missisauga Ojibway writer and minister; 1802-1856.

Jones, Peter; aka Pahtahsega: One Who Makes the World Brighter, or He Who Comes Shining; Mississauga Ojibway, Methodist minister; c1807-1890. Ojibway notable

Juniata: from Tyunayate: Projecting Rock. PA p.n.

- 𝒦 -

Kabemabe: Wet Mouth; 1837 t.s. Ojibway notable.

Kacheunishenawbay: Big Indian; 1863 t.s. Ojibway notable.

Kagiwigwan: Crow (or Raven's) Wing, or Raven Feather. MN p.n.

Kahaka (or Kakaquap): Sparrow; 1825, 1837 t.s. Ojibway notable.

Kahgegagahbowh: Stands Fast, Firm Standing, or He Who Stands Forever, aka George Copway; Mississauga Ojibway Methodist minister, writer; 1818-1869.

Kahkewaquonaby: Sacred Feathers. aka Peter Jones; writer and Methodist minister; 1802-1856. Mississauga notable.

Kakabeka Falls: River of Short Bends and Many Islands, or Always Plenty of Game. ON p.n.

Kakekapenais: Bird Forever; aka William Pennefeather (one Canadian treaty [CDN-124], signed in 1871, listed the signers as "Ojibway/Cree").

Kakiweonan: Land Crossing By Boat; aka Kewaunee: Wild Duck, or To Cross a Point, or Prairie Hen: WI p.n.

Kalamazoo, of Native origin, with several possible translations: It Smokes, Smoke, or Otter's Water; or from Kekekalakalamazoo: Where the Water Boils (or Smokes) in the Pot; or from Negikanamazo: Otter Tail, Beautiful Water, Boiling Water, or Stones Like Otters; or from Kikalamozo: He Is Inconvienced By Smoke In His Lodge. MI p.n.

Kalkaska: Burned Over. MI p.n.

Kanabec: Snake. MN p.n.

Kanadario: Sparkling Water; possible source of Ontario; or from Onitariio: Beautiful Lake; or from Ontarack: Rocks Standing High in the Water; other possible meanings: Great Lake, Beautiful Lake, Handsome Lake, or Large Lake; NY, OR, WI p.n.

Kanakee: from Tehyakkeki: Lowland, or Swampy Country. IN p.n.

Kanandawawinzo (ntg); aka LeBrocheux; 1837 t.s. Ojibway notable.

Kanapima: One Who Is Talked About; aka Augustin Hammelin, Jr.; 1813-?. Ottawa notable.

Kandiyohi: Buffalo Fish Come, or Where the Buffalo Fish Arrive. MN p.n.

Kaniekahaka (People of the Flint): Mohawk. or Gäneagaono (Possessors of the Flint).

Kanitareonto: Bay in the Lake, or Opening; possible source of Toronto: Fallen Trees in the Water, or Meeting Place; or from Deondo: Trees Growing Out of the Water; or from Thorontohen: Timbers on the Water. ON p.n.

Kanohquasa (ntg); aka William John; 1838 t.s. Onondaga notable.

Kapuskasing: from Paskeshegay: Rushing Water, or Shooting Water. ON p.n.

Kaqueticum: Snake; 1868 t.s. (CDN-18). Ojibway notable.

Karamanu: Walking Turtle; aka Nawkaw (ntg); 1735-1833. Winnebago notable.

Karbenequane: One Who Went in Front; 1815 t.s. Ottawa notable.

Karontaen: Coast of the Straits. Original name for Detroit. Also, Wawiyatanong: Where the River Turns, or Crooked Way; or Yondotiga: Great Village; MI p.n.

Karraymaunee: Walking Turtle; aka Tshuonuzheekau: He Who Stands in the House; 1829, 1832 t.s. Winnebago notable.

Kasabonika Lake: (ntg); First Nation of Ontario

Kasabonika: Lake with Many Islands, or Shallow Waterbed. Ontario First Nation.

Kashechewan: Swift Current. Ontario First Nation.

Kateri Tekakwitha: One Who Puts Things in Order, or She Hesitates; Mohawk holy woman made a Catholic Saint in 2012; 1656-1680. WI p.n.

Kaugaygeezhig: Everlasting Sky; 1837 t.s. Ojibway notable.

Kaukauna: from Okakaning: Fishing Place, or Crow-nesting Place, or Long Portage. WI p.n.

Kaurahkawseekan: Crow Killer; 1829 t.s. Winnebago notable.

Kaureekausawkaw: White Crow; 1828, 1832 t.s. Winnebago notable.

Kautawaubeta: Broken Tooth; 1825 t.s. Ojibway notable.

Kawachewan: Eddy; 1805 t.s. Ottawa notable.

Kawbemubbee: North Star; 1855 t.s. (aka Kobmubbey). Ojibway notable.

Kawwashkenekay: Crooked Arm; 1863 t.s. Ojibway notable.

Kaybaishcawdawway: Clear Round the Prairie; 1854 t.s. Ojibway notable.

Kaygwadaush: Attempter; 1855 t.s. Ojibway notable.

Kayrahtshokau: Clear Sky (or Clear Weather); 1828, 1829 t.s. Winnebago notable.

Kayraymaunee: Walking Turtle; 1829 t.s. Winnebago notable.

K-che-osauya: Elder Brother; 1837 t.s. Ojibway notable.

Kechewaishke: Buffalo; 1854 t.s. Ojibway notable.

Kechewametego: Big Frenchman; 1837 t.s. Ojibway notable.

Kechewawbeshayshe: Big Martin; 1854 t.s. Ojibway notable.

Keepers of the Sacred Fire: Potawatomi, or People of the Place of the Fire, or Fire Nation; responsible for the Three Fires Confederacy council fire; self-desig. Anishnabek: Original People, or Those Who Intend To Do Well (see Potawatomi). Michigan Tribe.

Keewatin: North Wind Place. MN, ON p.n.

Keewaygeeshig: Returning Sky; 1836 t.s. Ojibway notable.

Keewaywin: Going Home, or Going Back; First Nation of Ontario

Kehachiwinga: Wolf's Mountain Home Maker; aka Haksigaxunuminka: Little Fish Daughter; aka Mountain Wolf Woman; writer; 1884-1960. Winnebago notable.

Kehbehnawgay: Winner; 1863 t.s. Ojibway notable.

Kelystum: First Actor; 1815 t.s. Ottawa notable.

Kemenechagon: Bastard; 1815 t.s. Ottawa notable.

Kemewenaush: Raining Wind; 1863 t.s. Ojibway notable.

Kenatao: Cape; original name for Door County. WI p.n.

Kenogami: Long Water. ON p.n.

Kenora; a municipal name coined from KEewatin, NOrman, and RAt Portage. ON p.n.

Kenosha: Pickerel, or Pike. WI p.n.

Keshegekiaktakewum: Cedar Ridge; aka Cedar Point. WI p.n.

Keshena: Swift Flying Hawk. WI p.n.

Keueaghbon: Bald Eagle; 1818 t.s. Ottawa notable.

Kewaunee: To Cross a Point, Prairie Hen, or Wild Duck; or from Kakiweonan: Land Crossing By Boat. WI p.n.

Kewaydenogonaybe: Northern Feather; 1854 t.s. Ojibway notable.

Keweenaw: Cross A Point, or Portage. MI p.n.

Kewetakepe: All Around the Sky; 1825 t.s. Ojibway notable.

Kewetayash: Flying Around. (one Canadian treaty [CDN-124], signed in 1871, listed the signers as "Ojibway/Cree").

Keychepenayse: Big Bird; 1854 t.s. Ojibway notable.

Keynozhance: Little Jack Fish; 1854 t.s. Ojibway notable.

Kezhogowinninne: Skyman, Man of the Sky, or One Who Is Exalted; Mississauga; 1812-1889. Ojibway notable.

Khayratshoansaipkaw: Walks Naked; 1832 t.s. Winnebago notable.

Kiawatas: Tarrier; 1825 t.s. Ojibway notable.

Kickapoo: He Moves About. WI p.n.

Kineubenae: Golden Eagle; Mississauga; fl. 1797-1812 Ojibway notable.

King Hendrick; aka Theyanoguin: White Head; aka Hendrick Peters; sachem, diplomat; c1680-1755. Mohawk notable.

Kingfisher: First Nation of Ontario

Kinnickinnic: It Is Mixed (a smoking mixture of tobacco, sumac, and red willow). WI p.n.

Kino-gune-beek: (ntg): aka Louise Erdrich; writer, poet; 1954- Ojibway notable.

Kinongé: Pike; aka Le Brochet (Pike); fl. 1660-1713. Ottawa notable.

Kiotseaeton: The Hook; fl. 1645-46. Mohawk notable.

Kiskakon: Cut Tails, or Bear Clan; Nassauaketon: People of the Fork; Sable: Sandy Country People; Sinago: Squirrel Clan. Ottawa divisions.

Kisketawak: Cut Ear; 1837 t.s. Ojibway notable.

Kitchi-bitobigong: Grand Marais; Great Pond Place. MN p.n.

Kitchi-Gaugeedjiwunng: Great Falls; aka Niagara: Bisected Bottom Lands, Neck of Land Between Lakes, Thunder of Waters, or Resounding with Great Noise. ON p.n.

Kitchi-gummeng: Great Lake (of the Ojibway). Original name for Lake Superior. MI p.n.

Kitchi-Winigumeeng: Grand Portage. MN p.n.

Kithanne: Main Stream; source of Allegheny. PA p.n.

Kitiganisibi: Garden River. Ontario First Nation.

Kittanning: At the Big River, or Town on the Great River. PA p.n.

Kiwanis: Noise, or Noisy. WI p.n.

Knee: Nawagewa; 1837 t.s. Ojibway notable.

Koankaw: Chief; 1828 t.s. Winnebago notable.

Kobmubbey: North Star; 1863 t.s. (aka Kawbemubbee). Ojibway notable.

Kokomo: Black Walnut, or The Diver. IN p.n.

Komoka: Place Where the Dead Lie. ON p.n.

Konwatsi'tsiaienni: Someone Lends Her a Flower; aka Mary Brant; Clan Mother; c1736-1796. Mohawk notable.

Koocheching (ntg); First Nation of Ontario

Koochiching: Rainy Lake. MN p.n.

Koopoohoosha: (from) Red Wing: Wing of the Wild Swan Dyed Scarlet. MN p.n.

Korokoroheekaw: Bell; 1832 t.s. Winnebago notable.

Koshkonong: Closed in By Fog, or Hog Place. WI p.n.

Kuweukwanaku: Tall Pine Grove; original name for Philadelphia. PA p.n.

Kweeweezaishish (ntg); aka Gross Guelle; 1825 t.s. Ojibway notable.

- ℒ -

La Forte, Daniel; aka Hayouwaesh: Intestine Bruiser; 19th c. Chairman of the League of the Iroquois. Onondaga notable.

La Forte, Thomas; aka Shohehdonah: Large Feather; 19th c. Methodist minister. Onondaga notable.

La Pointe; originally Moningwonaekauning: Lapwing (or Plover) Land. WI p.n.

Lac des Mille Lacs: First Nation of Ontario

Lac du Flambeau: Lake of the Torches (a reference to a fishing method). WI reservation.

Lac La Croix: First Nation of Ontario

Lac Seul: First Nation of Ontario

Lackawanna: from Lechauhannek: Forks of the Stream. PA p.n.

Ladle: Choukeka; aka Spoon Decora; c1730-1816. Winnebago notable.

Lake Itasca, source of Mississippi; not of Native origin; named by Henry Rowe Schoolcraft from the Latin, verITAS CAput: "In Truth, The Head." MN p.n.

Lake of Beaver Meal Fragments: Wunnumin; or from Onumananing: Red Paint, or Vermillion. Ontario First Nation.

Lake of Calm Waters: Pikangikum. ON p.n.

Lake of the Torches (a reference to a fishing method): Lac du Flambeau:. WI reservation.

Lake Outlet, or Mouth of the River, or River Junction: Mendota. MN, WI p.n.

Lake River: Cuyahoga, or Important River, or Crooked River. OH p.n.

Lake St. Clair; orig. Wauwi-autinoong: Round Lake. MI p.n.

Lake Superior; orig. Kitchi-gummeng: Great Lake (of the Ojibway). MI p.n.

Lake with Many Islands, or Shallow Waterbed: Kasabonika. Ontario First Nation.

Land Covered with Moss: Nakina. ON p.n.

Land Crossing By Boat: Kakiweonan; aka Kewaunee: Wild Duck, or To Cross a Point, or Prairie Hen: WI p.n.

Land of Many Lakes: Minnesota - with several translations: Cloudy, Sky-colored, Whitish, or Milky Water; Water Reflecting Cloudy Skies; or Reflection of Sky on Water.

Land of Many River Islands: Gamanautigawaeyauk; original name for Thunder Bay: Animikie Wekwed. ON p.n.

Land Where the Partridge Drums: Akwesasne; aka St. Regis Reservation. Ontario First Nation.

Lapwing (or Plover) Land: Moningwonaekauning; original name for La Pointe. WI p.n.

Lapwing (or Plover) Place, or Golden-breasted Woodpecker Place: Moningwunkaning; original name for Madeline Is.; renamed after Chief White Crane's daughter. WI p.n.

Large and Beautiful: Chisago: from Kichisaga: or Large and Lovely Lake, or Large and Fair. MN p.n.

Large Feather: Shohehdonah; aka Thomas La Forte; 19th c. Methodist minister. Onondaga notable.

Large Lake; possible meaning of Ontario; or from Kanadario: Sparkling Water; or from Onitariio: Beautiful Lake; or from Ontarack: Rocks Standing High in the Water; other possible meanings: Great Lake, Beautiful Lake, or Handsome Lake; NY, WI p.n.

Large River: Maksrick-kitton; aka Delaware River, which was originally called Lenape Wihittuck: River of the Lenape. PA p.n.

Large River: Ohio, Beautiful River, or Fair to Look Upon, or simply Beautiful; other sources claim that the word is only a prefix meaning White Caps (or simply White). The full word for the river should then be Ohio-pek-hanne: River Whitened By Froth; or Ohiophanne: River Full of White Caps, or Very White River; also a CO, IL, IN, KY, NY, PA, WV place name.

Large Turtle Island (or Place of the Great Turtle): Mackinac (also spelled, and pronounced, Mackinaw): from Michilimackinak. MI p.n.

LaTrappe: aka Maghegabo (ntg); 1837 t.s. Ojibway notable.

LaTrappe: aka Niajegaboi (ntg); 1847 t.s. Ojibway notable.

Le Blanc, Jean; aka Outoutagan (ntg); fl. 1698-1712. Ottawa notable.

Le Brochet (Pike); aka Kinongé: Pike; fl. 1660-1713. Ottawa notable.

Le Grand Saulteur: Minweweh; aka Minavavana: The One with the Silver Tongue; c1710-1770. Ojibway notable.

Le Pesant: Heavy; aka Bear; fl. 1703-12. Ottawa notable.

Leader: Maugegabo; 1825 t.s. Ojibway notable.

Leading Feather: Nawgaunegwanabe; 1863, 1864 t.s. Ojibway notable.

Leather: Poshquaygin; 1854 t.s. Ojibway notable.

LeBrocheux: aka Kanandawawinzo; 1837 t.s. Ojibway notable.

Lechauhannek: Forks of the Stream; source of Lackawanna. PA p.n.

Lechauweeki: Where There Are Forks; source of Lehigh; or from Lechauwekink: At the Falls. PA p.n.

Lechauwekink: At the Falls; source of Lehigh; or from Lechauweeki: Where There Are Forks. PA p.n.

Leech Lake: from Gasagaskwajimekang: There Are Leeches There, or Full of Leeches. MN p.n.

Leek, or Garlic, or Onion; Chicacwa; source of Chicago; WI p.n.

Leek: Chicago; possibly from Chicacwa: Garlic, Onion, Leek, Onion Place, or Garlic Field. IL p.n.

Leelanau: Delight of Life; County given "Indian-sounding" name by Indian Agent Henry Rowe Schoolcraft, possibly meant to refer to Delight of Life. There is no "L" sound in the Ojibway language.). MI p.n.

Left-handed: Haynahahratshkay; 1829 t.s. Winnebago notable.

Legauihanne: Sandy Stream; source of Lycoming; or from Legawing: At the Place of Sand. PA p.n.

Lenape Wihittuck: River of the Lenape; orig. name for the Delaware River; aka Maksrick-kitton: Large River. PA p.n.

Lenape: Men of Our Nation, or Real People. PA p.n.

Lenawee: County given "Indian-sounding" name by Indian Agent Henry Rowe Schoolcraft, possibly meant to refer to "Man." There is no "L" sound in the Ojibway language. MI p.n.

Lenni Lenape: The Standard By Which All Men Are Measured. Ontario Tribe/First Nation; Wisconsin Tribe.

Les Chenaux; orig; Anaminang: In the Bowels (a reference to the channels' tortuous intricacy) . MI p.n.

Level Lands: Tuscola, or Warrior Prairie. MI p.n.

Light Falling on a Distant Object, or Bright Light: Wasso; 1837 t.s. Ojibway notable.

Little Abraham; aka Teiorhenhsere (ntg); -1780. Mohawk notable.

Little Bear: Macquettequet; 1805, 1807 t.s. Ojibway notable.

Little Beef: Pugaagik; 1825 t.s. Ojibway notable.

Little Boy Child: Hakahkah; 1837 t.s. Winnebago notable.

Little Buck: Iaubensee; 1825 t.s. Ojibway notable.

Little Cedar: Meuetugesheck; 1807 t.s. Ojibway notable.

Little Chief (ie, chief of subordinate authority): Ogimaus; 1837 t.s. Ojibway notable. Okemos. MI p.n.

Little Chief (or Little Priest) Hoonkhoonokaw; 1855 t.s. Winnebago notable.

Little Chief: Okemas; 1815 t.s. Ottawa notable.

Little Current: Nawwawgewawnose; 1854 t.s. Ojibway notable.

Little Current; aka Waibejewung: Place Where the Waters Flow Back and Forth. ON p.n.

Little Decora; aka Mawhecooshawnawzhekaw: One that Stands And Reaches the Sky; 1797-1887; 1855 t.s. Winnebago notable.

Little Elk: Hoowauneekaw (or Howamicka); 1825, 1828, 1829, 1832 t.s. Winnebago notable.

Little Englishman: Shawgawnawsheence; 1854 t.s. Ojibway notable.

Little Fish Daughter: Haksigaxunuminka; aka Kehachiwinga: Wolf's Mountain Home Maker; aka Mountain Wolf Woman; writer; 1884-1960. Winnebago notable.

Little Fly: Menactome; 1815 t.s. Ojibway notable.

Little Fox: Wahgoshig First Nation (Ontario)

Little Frenchman: Wametegoshins; 1837 t.s. Ojibway notable.

Little Frolic: Pocohontas. PA p.n.

Little Hill: Shogonickah; 1837, 1855 t.s. Winnebago notable.

Little Hill: Waudekaw; 1855 t.s. Ojibway notable.

Little Jack Fish: Keynozhance; 1854 t.s. Ojibway notable.

Little Ottawa: Ottawaus; 1837 t.s. Ojibway notable.

Little Otter: Nekeik; 1805 t.s. Ottawa notable.

Little Otter: Toshunukhohonik (or Toshunuckah); 1832, 1837 t.s. Winnebago notable.

Little Priest: Morahtshaykaw (or Morachaykah); 1828, 1832, 1837 t.s. Winnebago notable.

Little Reindeer: Awdekonse; 1854 t.s. Ojibway notable.

Little Rock: Aseenewub; 1863, 1864 t.s. Ojibway notable.

Little Round Hill: Wadena. MN p.n.

Little Shell: Aseanse; 1863 t.s. Ojibway notable.

Little Shoe: Bwaness; 1864 t.s. Ojibway notable.

Little Six: Shagobai; 1837 t.s. Ojibway notable.

Little Snake: Wakaunhononickah; 1832, 1837 t.s. Winnebago notable.

Little Soldier: Manapaykah; 1837 t.s. Winnebago notable.

Little Thunder: Nemekas; 1795, 1807 t.s. Ojibway notable.

Little Thunder: Wakunchanickah; 1837 t.s. Winnebago notable.

Little Thunder: Wawhecoochawhoonokaw; 1855 t.s. Winnebago notable.

Little Walker: Wauneehononik; 1832 t.s. Winnebago notable.

Little White Bear: Mauntshanigeenig; 1829 t.s. Winnebago notable.

Loft, John; aka Hearenhodoh: Standing Tree; 19th c. leader. Mohawk notable.

Lone Man: Byeajick or Payajik; 1837, 1854 t.s. Ojibway notable.

Long Bay or Strait, or South Portage: Shawanaga First Nation. ON p.n.

Long Knife (name for Americans): Chemokcomon; 1817 t.s. Ojibway notable.

Long Lake 77 First Nation; now known as Ginoogaming First Nation (Ontario)

Long Lake: First Nation of Ontario

Long Narrow Strip of Land Running Into the Water: Chequamegon: from Shaugauwaumekong. WI p.n.

Long Portage, or Fishing Place, or Crow-nesting Place: Okakaning; source of Kaukauna. WI p.n.

Long Water: Kenogami. ON p.n.

Long, Open Channel: Maganetewan. ON p.n.

Long: Guneu; source of Conoy. PA p.n.

Longhouse, People of the: Haudenosaunee; aka Iroquois: from Algonquin Irinakhoiw: Rattlesnakes. Ontario Tribe/First Nation.

Long-tailed: Erie, or Panther. NY p.n.; OH p.n.; ON p.n.

Loon's Foot: Monga-zid or Manggosit or Mawngosit; 1825, 1837, 1854 t.s. Ojibway notable.

Lost Dauphin of France (claimed to be the): Williams, Eleazar; aka Onwarenhiiaki: Tree Cutter; controversial preacher; 1788-1858. Mohawk notable.

Lost River: Manistee (and Manistique). or Crooked River, or Red River, or Wind Sound, or Wood's Spirit. MI p.n.

Lowland: Kanakee. from Tehyakkeki:, or Swampy Country. IN p.n.

Lycoming: from Legauihanne: Sandy Stream, or from Legawing: At the Place of Sand. PA p.n.

- *M* -

Mackinac (also spelled, and always pronounced, Mackinaw): from Michilimackinak; Large Turtle Island, or Place of the Great Turtle. MI p.n.

Mackinac Bands of Ottawa and Chippewa Indians: State-recognized Tribe of Michigan.

Macouda: Bear's Heart; 1837 t.s. Ojibway notable.

Macoupin: Potato. IL p.n.

Macquettequet: Little Bear; 1805, 1807 t.s. Ojibway notable.

Macungy: Feeding Place of Bears. PA p.n.

Madawaska: Grassy River Mouth. ON p.n.

Madeline Is.; orig. Moningwunkaning: Lapwing Place, or Golden-breasted Woodpecker Place; renamed after Chief White Crane's daughter. WI p.n.

Madison; orig. Dejop: Four Lakes. WI p.n.

Maganetewan: Long, Open Channel. ON p.n.

Maghegabo (ntg); aka LaTrappe; 1837 t.s. Ojibway

Magnetawan: Swiftly Flowing Waters; First Nation of Ontario

Mahanoy: Salt Lick. PA p.n.

Mahican: Wolf; or from Muh-heconneok: People of the Waters that Are Never Still (a reference to the Hudson River). WI tribe (see below).

Mahican; aka Stockbridge-Munsee; an amalgamated tribe of Stockbridge people made up of Mahican and other Algonkian, and the Munsee who are a Delaware subgroup. Moved by the government to Wisconsin from the northeast in the 1840s. WI tribe.

Mahnomen: Wild Rice. MN p.n.

Main River, or Cold, Clear Water: Neosho. WI p.n.

Main Stream: Kithanne; source of Allegheny. PA p.n.

Maisaninnine: Stylish Person; aka Zhuawuno-geezhigo-gaubow: He Who Stands in the Southern Sky; aka; Jack Fiddler; c1830-1907. Ojibway notable.

Makato River: from Makato Osa Watapa: River Where Blue Earth Is Gathered. MN p.n.

Makes the Ground Tremble: Sasagohcumickishcum; 1864 t.s. Ojibway notable.

Maksrick kitton: Large River; aka Delaware River, which was originally called Lenape Wihittuck: River of the Lenape. PA p.n.

Male Devil: Manitonobe; 1868 t.s. (CDN 18) Ojibway notable.

Mamaushegauta: Bad Legs; 1807 t.s. Ojibway notable.

Man Eater: Woankshikrootshkay; 1829 t.s. Winnebago notable.

Man Eaters, or Cannibals: Mohawk. Ontario Tribe/First Nation.

Man of the Sky: Kezhogowinninne: or Skyman, or One Who Is Exalted; Mississauga; 1812 1889. Ojibway notable.

Man Shooting at the Mark: Paashineep; 1825 t.s. Ojibway notable.

Man that Stands First: Natamegabo; 1837 t.s. Ojibway notable.

Man: Illinois, from Illini: plural, Illiniwok: People, or Perfect and Accomplished Men; Illinois divisions: Cahokia (ntg), and Tamaroa: He Has a Cut Tail; Oklahoma tribe

Man: Lenawee; County given "Indian-sounding" name by Indian Agent Henry Rowe Schoolcraft, possibly meant to refer to "Man." There is no "L" sound in the Ojibway language. MI p.n.

Manahkeetshumpkaw: Spotted Arm; 1828 t.s. Winnebago notable.

Manapaykah: Little Soldier; 1837 t.s. Winnebago notable.

Man-eaters (or Cannibals): MOHAWK; possibly from Mohowauuck: They Eat Animate Things; also translated as Keepers of the Eastern Door. several self designations; Ongwe howe: Real People, Cannieigas: Flint People, Kanien'kéhaka: People of the Flint, and Gäneagaono: Possessors of the Flint; New York, Ontario, Quebec tribe (the Akwesasne Mohawk are of New York); part of the Iroquois confederacy; all of Mohawk territory is called Kanienkeh: Land of the Flint.

Manggosit: Loon's Foot; 1837 t.s. Ojibway notable.

Manhattan: Hilly Island, or Bow and Arrow Wood Place. PA p.n.

Manistee (and Manistique): Crooked River, Red River, Wind Sound, Lost River, or Wood's Spirit. MI p.n.

Manitobininince: Devil's Bird; 1868 t.s. (CDN 18). Ojibway notable.

Manitonobe: Male Devil; 1868 t.s. (CDN 18) Ojibway notable.

Manitou: Spirit (often translated as "devil"; see above). MI p.n.

Manitoulin: Island of the Spirit; or a corruption of Manitowaning: At the Spirit's Cave; ON p.n.

Manitowaning: At the Spirit's Cave, or Great Spirit Cave; possibly corrupted from Manitoulin: Island of the Spirit; ON p.n.

Manitowoc: River of Bad Spirits, or Spirit Land. WI p.n.

Mankato: Blue Earth, or Earth Paint Pigment (site of largest mass execution in U.S. history, where 38 Dakota were hanged on Dec. 26, 1862); (See p.42 for list of those hung); MN p.n.

Manotokeshick: Spirit of the Day; 1863 t.s. Ojibway notable.

Many Fish River: Ashtabula, or Always Enough Fish Moving in the River. OH p.n.

Marigold, or White Feather: Wabigoon First Nation (Ontario)

Marked Legs: Peshekata; 1818 t.s. Ottawa notable.

Marsh: Skokie. IL p.n.

Marten Falls: First Nation of Ontario

Martin, Peter; aka Oronhyatekha: Burning Cloud; physician, author; 1841-1907. Mohawk notable.

Mashipinashiwish: Bad Bird; 1795 t.s. Ojibway notable.

Maski Sebi: Swamp River, original name; aka Bad River, from Masshki zeebi; ("maski" was mistook for "matchi," so we get Bad, not Swamp). WI p.n.

Matachewan: Meeting of the Currents; First Nation of Ontario

Matachewan: River Current Is Heard. Ontario First Nation.

Match-e-be-nash-she-wish Band of Pottawatomi Indians: Bad Bird; (aka Gun Lake Tribe). Michigan Reservation

Mattagami: Meeting of the Currents; First Nation of Ontario

Mattawa: River Flowing Into Another Body of Water, or Where the Current Begins, or River Flowing Into the Lake. ON p.n.

Matwaash: Heard Fell Down; 1817 t.s. Ojibway notable.

Maugegabo, or Maugegawbow: Leader, Stepping Ahead; 1825, 1855 t.s. Ojibway notable.

Mauheeherkarrah: Flying Cloud; 1832 t.s. Winnebago notable.

Maukeewukkaw: Cloudy; 1832 t.s. Winnebago notable.

Maumee: People of the Peninsula; or from Meahme: All Friends (source of Miami). IN, OH p.n.

Maunahpeykaw: Soldier; 1832 t.s. Winnebago notable.

Mauneehatakau: Big Walker; 1829 t.s. Winnebago notable.

Maungeezik: Big Foot; 1828 t.s. Winnebago notable.

Maunkawkaw: Earth; 1829 t.s. Winnebago notable.

Maunkkayraykau: Crooked Tail; 1829 t.s. Winnebago notable.

Maunkshawka: White Breast; 1829 t.s. Winnebago notable.

Mauntshanigeenig: Little White Bear; 1829 t.s. Winnebago notable.

Maushoatshkaw: Blue Earth; 1832 t.s. Winnebago notable.

Mauwauruck: Muddy; 1832 t.s. Winnebago notable.

Mawcawday: Bear's Heart; 1854 t.s. Ojibway notable.

Mawcawdaywawquot: Black Cloud; 1854 t.s. Ojibway notable.

Mawhecooshawnawzhekaw: One that Stands And Reaches the Sky; aka Little Decora; 1797-1887; 1855 t.s. Winnebago notable.

Mawjekeshick: Travelling Sky; 1863 t.s. Ojibway notable.

Mawngosit: Loon's Foot; 1854 t.s. Ojibway notable.

Maxatawny: Bear Path, or Bear's Path Stream. PA p.n.

Mayajewaywedung: Chorister; 1855, 1863 t.s. Ojibway notable.

Maydwaguanonind: He that Is Spoken To; 1864 t.s. Ojibway notable.

Mayshueeyaush (or Mayzhakeosh): Dropping Wind; 1863, 1864 t.s. Ojibway notable.

Mayzin: Checkered; 1836 t.s. Ojibway notable.

McArthur: aka Tashcuygon (ntg); 1815 t.s. Ottawa notable.

McCarty: aka Tushquagon (ntg); 1805, 1818 t.s. Ottawa notable.

McCarty: Misquegin (ntg); 1817 t.s. Ottawa notable.

McCoonse, Francis, aka Eshtonoquot: Clear Sky; 1836, 1859 t.s. Ojibway notable.

McDowell Lake: First Nation of Ontario

M'chevomi: Extensive Flats; source of Wyoming. PA p.n.

M'Chigeeng: Village Enclosed by Stepped Cliffs; First Nation of Ontario

Mcokenuh: Bear King; 1814 t.s. Ottawa notable.

Mdewakanton Dakota: Sacred Mystery Lake Village. Minnesota tribe.

Meadow Sparrow: Mushkootagwima, or Feather in the Meadow; 1837 t.s. Ojibway notable.

Mechimenduch: Big Bowl; 1805 t.s. Ottawa notable.

Mecosta: Bear Cub. MI p.n.

Medicine Man: Saguima; fl. 1707-44. Ottawa notable.

Meeting of the Currents: Matachewan First Nation (Ontario)

Meeting of the Currents: Mattagami First Nation (Ontario)

Meeting Place, or Fallen Trees in the Water: Toronto; or from Deondo: Trees Growing Out of the Water; or from Kanitareonto: Bay in the Lake, or Opening; or from Thorontohen: Timbers on the Water. ON p.n.

Mejawkekeshick: Sky that Touches the Ground; 1863 t.s. Ojibway notable.

Men of Our Nation, or Real People: Lenape. PA p.n.

Men of the Good Seed (Wild Rice): Menominee. WI tribe.

Menachksink: Where There Is a Fort; original name for Pittsburgh. PA p.n.

Menactome: Little Fly; 1815 t.s. Ojibway notable.

Menaun gehilla: River with Banks that Fall Down; possible source of Monongahela: River Digging Away Its Shores, or River with Sliding Banks; PA p.n.

Mendota: Mouth of the River, River Junction, or Lake Outlet. MN, WI p.n.

Mene-awkee; Good Earth, or Rich Land; aka Milwaukee; or from Mino-aki: Fair, Fertile Land. WI p.n.

Menitugawboway: Devil Standing; 1815 t.s. Ottawa notable.

Menkayraykan: Spotted Earth; 1828 t.s. Winnebago notable.

Mennekam: Bear Who Scratches; 1829 t.s. Winnebago notable.

Menogeshick: Fine Day; 1863 t.s. Ojibway notable.

Menominee: Wild Rice People. Men of the Good Seed (Wild Rice). WI tribe. MI p.n.

Menomineekeshen: Rice maker; 1863 t.s. Ojibway notable.

Merchant: Wanonchequa; 1825 t.s. Winnebago notable.

Mermaid: Nebonabee; 1825 t.s. Ojibway notable.

Merrimac: Fish (sturgeon or catfish). WI p.n.

Mesabi: Giant, or Hidden Giant (Iron Range name). MN p.n.

Meshenawway: Disciple; 1854 t.s. Ojibway notable.

Meskousing: Where the Waters Gather, Place of the Red Earth People, or Red Stone; possible source of Wisconsin: with possible meanings: Muskrat Land, Grassy Place; or from Misconsin: Strong Current; or from Weeskonsan: Gathering of the Waters.

Mesquab (ntg): aka Johnathan Yorke; artist; fl. 1900s. Ojibway notable.

Metesheneiwa: Bear's Man; 1818 t.s. Ottawa notable.

Meuetugesheck: Little Cedar; 1807 t.s. Ojibway notable.

Mexico (from the Aztec): Place of the War God. OH, PA p.n.

Miami: from Meahme (or Wemiamik): All Friends; aka the Pahkah Miami: or from Omaumeg: People who Live on the Peninsula (a reference to the Door Peninsula,WI); or Beautiful Miami; self desig. Twightwee, or Twatwa: Cry of the Crane. Indiana, Wisconsin tribe: IN, OH p.n.

MICHIGAN - most often translated as Big Lake; as in Michi (big) and Gammi (lake); or Mishi-gummeeng: Great Body of Water; other translations found were Majigan: Clearing, Majiigan: Large Clearing, and Mishi-maikin: Swimming Turtle; used as a place name throughout the Midwest.

Michilimackinak; Large Turtle Island or Place of the Great Turtle: Mackinac (also spelled, and always pronounced, Mackinaw). MI p.n.

Michipicoten: Big Bluffs, Bold Promontories Place, or Broken, Craggy Highlands Place. First Nation of Ontario; ON p.n.

Migisi: Eagle; aka Dokis; aka Michel d'Aigle; c1818-1906; 1854, 1855 t.s.; Ontario First Nation. Ojibway notable.

Mikinak: Turtle; ?-1755. Ottawa notable.

Mille Lacs; orig. Mishi sagaigun: Big Lake; originally the home of the Santee Sioux. MN p.n. Minn-esota Ojibway Reservation.

Milwaukee: from Mene-awkee; Good Earth, or Rich Land; or from Mino-aki: Fair, Fertile Land. WI p.n.

Mimico: Wild Pigeon Place. ON p.n.

Mindemoya (Lake): Old Woman Lake. ON p.n.

Minduwahwing: Berry Hunter; 1863 t.s. Ojibway notable.

Mink: Onqueess; 1825 t.s. Ojibway notable.

Mink: Shawfauwick; 1825 t.s. Ottawa notable.

Minneapolis: Water (or Waterfall) City: from the Sioux Minne plus the Greek apolis (city). MN p.n.

MINNESOTA, with several translations: Cloudy, Sky colored, Whitish, or Milky Water; Water Reflecting Cloudy Skies; Reflection of Sky on Water; or Land of Many Lakes.

Minnetonka: Big Water. MN p.n.

Mino-aki: Fair, Fertile Land: Milwaukee; or from Mene awkee; Good Earth, or Rich Land. WI p.n.

Mintougaboit: Devil Standing; 1817 t.s. Ojibway notable.

Miscoconoya: Red Rob; 1863 t.s. Ojibway notable.

Miscomukquah: Red Bear; 1863, 1864 t.s. Ojibway notable.

Misconsin: Strong Current; possible source of Wisconsin: possible meanings: Muskrat Land, Grassy Place; or from Meskousing: Where the Waters Gather, Place of the Red Earth People, or Red Stone; or from Weeskonsan: Gathering of the Waters.

Miscopenenshay: Red Bird; 1863 t.s. Ojibway notable.

Mishi sagaigun: Mille Lacs; Big Lake; originally the home of the Santee Sioux. MN p.n.

Mishkeegogamang: (formerly known as Osnaburgh First Nation of Ontario); First Nation of Ontario

Miskookenew: Red Eagle; aka Henry Prince. (one Canadian treaty [CDN 124], signed in 1871, listed the signers as "Ojibway/Cree").

Miskwagamiwi sagaigun (from): Red Lake; or Red watered Lake. Minnesota reservation.

Misquadace: Turtle; 1864 t.s. Ojibway notable.

Misquegin (ntg): aka McCarty; 1817 t.s. (see Tushquagon). Ottawa notable.

Missabe (Iron Range): Giant. MN, WI p.n.

Missanabie Cree: Pictured Water; First Nation of Ontario

Missaukee: At the Big Outlet. MI p.n.

Missinaibi: Pictures on the Water (reference to pictographs along banks). ON p.n.

Mississauga: River Having Many Outlets; an Ojibway subdivision, of Ontario. Newer documents group them as Ojibway; First Nation of Ontario; ON p.n.

Mississaugas of Scugog Island: Swampy or Marshy Land; First Nation of Ontario

Mississaugas of the Credit: First Nation of Ontario

Mississinewa: Big Stone River. OH p.n.

Mitaanjigamiing: Where Shallow Water Runs into Deep Water; First Nation of Ontario: new name for Stanjikoming (a true misnomer; a word with no meaning in any language)

Mitchigee-waedinong: Bare West Place; aka West Bay (Manitoulin Is). Ontario First Nation.

Mocreebec Indian Government: First Nation of Ontario

Modoc: from Shasteeca, word for Enemy. IN p.n.

MOHAWK: most often translated as Man-eaters, or Cannibals; possibly from Mohowauuck: They Eat Animate Things; also translated as Keepers of the Eastern Door. several self designations; Ongwe howe: Real People, Cannieigas: Flint People, Kanien'kéhaka: People of the Flint, and Gäneagaono: Possessors of the Flint; New York, Ontario, Quebec tribe (the Akwesasne Mohawk are of New York); part of the Iroquois confederacy; all of Mohawk territory is called Kanienkeh: Land of the Flint.

Mohawk territory: Kanienkeh; Land of the Flint; NY; ON; Que.

Mohawks of Akwesasne; First Nation of Ontario

Mohawks of the Bay of Quinte; First Nation of Ontario

Monga zid: Loon's Foot; 1825 t.s. Ojibway notable.

Monimack: Catfish; 1805 t.s. Ojibway notable.

Moningwunkaning: Golden breasted Woodpecker Place, or Lapwing Place; original name for Madeline Is.; renamed after Chief White Crane's daughter. WI p.n.

Monongahela: River Digging Away Its Shores, or River with Sliding Banks; or from Menaungehilla: River with Banks that Fall Down. PA p.n.

Monsomo: Moose Dung; 1863 t.s. Ojibway notable.

Montagnais: Mountaineers (French); self desig. Neenoilno: Perfect People, or Innu People. Ontario Tribe/First Nation.

Montsomo: Murdering Yell; 1837 t.s. Ojibway notable.

Moose Cree: First Nation of Ontario

Moose Deer Point: First Nation of Ontario

Moose Dung: Monsomo; 1863 t.s. Ojibway notable.

Moose: Moseomannay; 1863 t.s. Ojibway notable.

Moose: Mosinee. WI p.n.

Mooseomone: Plenty of Elk; 1825 t.s. Ojibway notable.

Morahtshaykaw (or Morachaykah): Little Priest; 1828, 1832, 1837 t.s. Winnebago notable.

Morrisseau, Norval: aka Copper Thunderbird; Ojibway artist; 1932-2007.

Moseomannay: Moose; 1863 t.s. Ojibway notable.

Mosinee: Moose. WI p.n.

Mountain Traveler: Babawmadjeweshcang; 1866 t.s. Ojibway notable.

Mountain Wolf Woman; aka Haksigaxunuminka: Little Fish Daughter; aka Kehachiwinga: Wolf's Mountain Home Maker; writer; 1884-1960. Winnebago notable.

Mountaineers (French): Montagnais; self desig. Neenoilno: Perfect People, or Innu People. Ontario Tribe/First Nation.

Mouth of the River, or Yellow Earth Place: Ozaukee. WI p.n.

Mouth of the River, River Junction, or Lake Outlet: Mendota. WI p.n.

Mouth of the River: Saugeen. Ojibway First Nation; Ontario p.n.

Moving Sun: Garakonthie; aka Daniel; peace leader; 1600-1676. Onondaga notable.

Mucky Land (people at): Cayuga: Gweugwehono (People at the Mucky Land), or Siotino-nawentowane (People of the Big Pipe).

Muddy Bottom, or Submerged Land: Scugog. ON p.n.

Muddy River: Susquehanna; or from Guneshachachgak-hanne: Great Bend River. PA p.n.

Muddy: Mauwauruck; 1832 t.s. Winnebago notable.

Muheconneok: People of the Waters that Are Never Still (a reference to the Hudson River); aka Mahican: Wolf. WI tribe.

Mukkukoosh: Broken Chest (or keg, box); 1837 t.s. Ojibway notable.

Muncie: Stone Country People. IN p.n.

Munising: Island in the Lake. MI p.n.

Munominekayshein: Rice Maker; 1855 t.s. Ojibway

Munsee: People of the Stoney Country; aka Muncie; Delaware/Lenni Lenape sub tribe; Pennsylvania, Wisconsin tribe. The Stockbridge Munsee are an amalgamated tribe of Stockbridge people made up of Mahican, and other Algonkians, and the Munsee. Moved by the government to Wisconsin from the northeast in the 1840s.

Munsee-Delaware Nation: First Nation of Ontario

Munuscong: Place of the Reeds. MI p.n.

Murdering Yell: Montsomo; 1837 t.s. Ojibway notable.

Muscatatuck: Clear River. IN p.n.

Mushkoas: Elk; 1825 t.s. Ojibway notable.

Mushkootagwima: Meadow Sparrow, or Feather in the Meadow; 1837 t.s. Ojibway notable.

Muskegon: Swampy, or Marshy River; or from Maskegowok: Swamp People. MI p.n.

Muskigonce: Swamp; 1868 t.s. (CDN 18). Ojibway notable.

Muskingum: By the River. OH p.n.

Muskoka: Red Earth. ON p.n.

Muskrat Dam Lake: First Nation of Ontario

Muskrat Land, or Grassy Place: possible meanings of Wisconsin ; or from Meskousing: Where the Waters Gather, Place of the Red Earth People, or Red Stone; or from Misconsin: Strong Current; or from Weeskonsan: Gathering of the Waters.

Muskrat: Shwanabe; 1818 t.s. Ottawa notable.

Musquakie: Yellow Head; 1868 t.s. (CDN 18). Ojibway notable.

Musquakie; aka William Yellowhead; d.1864 (possible father to previous). Ojibway notable.

Myyawgewaywedunk: One Who Carries the Voice; 1854 t.s. Ojibway notable.

- *N* -

Nabineashe: Bird that Flies on One Side; 1847 t.s. Ojibway notable.

Nahnebahwequay: Upright Woman; Ojibway activist; 1824 1865.

Naicatchewenin: At the Place Where the Current is Obstructed; First Nation of Ontario

Nail, Hoof, or Claw: Oshkosh; Menominee; 1795-1858. WI p.n.

Nakina: Land Covered with Moss. ON p.n.

Namaygoosisagagun: Trout Lake (non-Status); First Nation of Ontario

Name Bearers: Hodiseññageta; aka the ONONDAGA: from Onundägaono: People on (Top of) the Hills, or from Onontakehaka: People of the Hill; New York, Ontario tribe; part of the Iroquois Confederacy; NY p.n.

Namekagon: Sturgeon Place. WI p.n.

Nanawananaw: Centre of Bird's Tail (one Canadian treaty [CDN 124], signed in 1871, listed the signers as "Ojibway/Cree").

Nangotuck: Flame; 1825 t.s. Ojibway notable.

Nankaw: Wood; 1828 t.s. Winnebago notable.

Nanticoke: Tide water. ON, PA p.n.

Naotkamegwanning Anishinabe: Of the Whitefish Point; First Nation of Ontario

Napanee: Flour. ON p.n.

Naquanabie: Feather; 1837 t.s. Ojibway notable.

Narrows Separating Two Lakes, At the Edge of a Whirlpool, or, Group of Pine Trees: Couchiching. Ontario First Nation.

Nashake: Flying Down Bird (one Canadian treaty [CDN 124], signed in 1871, listed the signers as "Ojibway/Cree").

Nashua: Beautiful River with Pebbly Bottom. MN p.n.

Nassauaketon: People of the Fork; Kiskakon: Cut Tails, or Bear Clan; Sable: Sandy Country People; Sinago: Squirrel Clan. Ottawa divisions.

Natamegabo: Man that Stands First; 1837 t.s. Ojibway notable.

Natgeeshig: Driving Clouds; 1836 t.s. Ojibway notable.

Nathkaysawkaw: Fierce Heart; 1828 t.s. Winnebago notable.

Naudin: Wind; 1825, 1837 t.s. Ojibway notable.

Naugaunosh: Forward Man; 1825 t.s. Ojibway notable.

Naukawkarymaunie: Wood; 1829 t.s. Winnebago notable.

Nautchkaysuck: Quick Heart; 1829, 1837 t.s. Winnebago notable.

Nautshkaypeenkaw: Good Heart; 1832 t.s. Winnebago notable.

Nawagewa: Knee; 1837 t.s. Ojibway notable.

Nawahjegezhegwabe: Sloping Sky; aka Joseph Sawyer; Ojibway Grand Chief; 1786-1863. Ojibway notable.

Nawboneaush: Young Man's Son; 1863 t.s. (see Naybunacaush, below). Ojibway notable.

Nawgaunegwanabe: Leading Feather; 1863, 1864 t.s. Ojibway notable.

Nawgawnegawbow: One Standing Ahead; 1863 t.s. Ojibway notable.

Nawgawnub: Foremost Sitter; 1854 t.s. Ojibway notable.

Nawkaw (ntg); aka Karamanu: Walking Turtle; 1735-1833. Winnebago notable.

Nawtawmegezhick: First Sky; 1854 t.s. Ojibway notable.

Nawwawgewawnose: Little Current; 1854 t.s. Ojibway notable.

Naybunacaush: Young Man's Son; 1855 t.s. (see Nawboneaush, above). Ojibway notable.

Naynawonggaybe: Dressing Bird; 1854 t.s. Ojibway notable.

Nebacoim: Night Thunder; 1847 t.s. Ojibway notable.

Nebenequingwahawegaw: Summer Wolverine; 1863 t.s. Ojibway notable.

Nebonabee: Mermaid; 1825 t.s. Ojibway notable.

Necedah: Yellow. WI p.n.

Neck of Land Between Lakes, Bisected Bottom Lands, Thunder of Waters, or Resounding with Great Noise: Niagara: aka Kitchi Gaugeedjiwunng: Great Falls. ON p.n.

Neck of Land Between Lakes: Niagara. WI p.n.

Neebing: Summer. ON p.n.

Neechahkekoonahonah: Where the Rocks Strike Together; original name for Wisconsin Dells. WI p.n.

Needle, Awl, Disappearing River, Noise Underground, Reed-like, Thundering Under the Ground, or Something that Pierces: Sheboygan; or from Shabwawagoning: Rumbling Waters, or Waters Disappearing Underground. WI p.n.

Neehookaw: Whirlpool; 1828 t.s. Winnebago notable.

Neenah: Running Water. WI p.n.

Neenoilno: Innu People, or Perfect People; self. desig. of the Montagnais: Mountaineers (French). Ontario Tribe/First Nation.

Neesidaysish: Sky; 1825 t.s. Ojibway notable.

Neesopena: Two Birds; 1825 t.s. Ojibway notable.

Negaunee: He Walks Ahead (ie. the pioneer). MI p.n.

Negig: Otter; 1807 t.s. Ojibway notable.

Negig: Otter; 1854 t.s. Ojibway notable.

Neiyosheonegaming (ntg): aka Cape Croker; Ontario First Nation

Nekeik: Little Otter; 1805 t.s. Ottawa notable.

Nemekas: Little Thunder; 1795, 1807 t.s. Ojibway notable.

Neokeshick: Four Skies; 1863 t.s. Ojibway notable.

Neoning: Four Fingers; 1866 t.s. Ojibway notable.

Neosho: Cold, Clear Water, or Main River. WI p.n.

Neshannock: Double Stream. PA p.n.

Neskantaga: (ntg) First Nation of Ontario

Netmizaaggamig Nishnaabeg: (ntg) formerly Pic Mobert First Nation of Ontario

New Post: former name for Taykwa Tagamou (ntg) First Nation (Ontario)

Neyashewun: Point of Land; source of Thessalon First Nation (Ontario)

Niagara: Bisected Bottom Lands, Neck of Land Between Lakes, Thunder of Waters, or Resounding with Great Noise; aka Kitchi Gaugeedjiwunng: Great Falls. ON, WI p.n.

Niajegaboi (ntg): aka LaTrappe; 1847 t.s. Ojibway notable.

Night that Meets: Haunheighkeepawkaw; 1832 t.s. Winnebago notable.

Night Thunder: Nebacoim; 1847 t.s. Ojibway notable.

Nigowidjiw: Sand Mountain. Grand Sable Dunes. MI p.n.

Niisaachewan Anishinaabe Nation: (ntg) First Nation of Ontario

Nine Fingers: Changasoning; 1847 t.s. Ojibway notable

Nipigon: So Long that You Cannot See the End of It; or from Animibeegoong: Along the Water's Edge, or Continuous Water. ON p.n.

Nipisisinan: Little Body of Water (ie. the smallest of the Great Lakes); aka Lake Nipissing: In a Little Water, At the Place of the Waters or, In the Leaves. ON p.n.

Nipissing (Lake): At the Place of the Waters; or In a Little Water, or In the Leaves; or from Little Body of Water (ie. the smallest of the Great Lakes): from Nipisisinan. First Nation of Ontario

Nisiwaurooshkun: Bear; 1829 t.s. Winnebago notable.

Nissodjiwunaung: Three Channels: aka Walpole Island (Unceded Indian Territory). Ontario First Nation.

Nissowaquet: Forked River; c1715-1797. Ottawa notable.

Noise of Water Far Away is Heard: Petawawa. ON p.n.

Noise Underground, Needle, Awl, Disappearing River, Reed Like, Thundering Under the Ground, or Something that Pierces: Sheboygan; or from Shabwawagoning: Rumbling Waters, or Waters Disappearing Underground. WI p.n.

Noise, or Noisy: Kiwanis. WI p.n.

Noisy Stream Flowing Over, or Roaring Stream: Ganshowehanne; original name for Schuylkill: Hidden River (perhaps a Dutch word and not Native at all). PA p.n.

North Caribou Lake: First Nation of Ontario

North Spirit Lake: First Nation of Ontario

North Star: Kawbemubbee. (aka Kobmubbey); 1855, 1863 t.s. Ojibway notable.

North Wind Place: Keewatin. MN, ON p.n.

Northern Feather: Kewaydenogonaybe; 1854 t.s. Ojibway notable.

Northwest Angle No. 33: First Nation of Ontario

Northwest Angle No. 37: First Nation of Ontario

Norton, Major John: aka Teyoninhokerawen (ntg); fl. 1784-1825. Mohawk notable.

Nowacumig: At the Center of the Universe; aka Dennis Banks; co-founder of the American Indian Movement. 1937-2017. Ojibway notable.

Nowgeshick: Twelve O'clock; 1815 t.s. Ojibway notable.

Nundawaono: Great Hill People, self. desig. of the Seneca. Ontario Tribe/First Nation.

Nunqueweebee: Thunder Sitting; 1828 t.s. Winnebago notable.

- *O* -

Obahbahm wawagezhegoqua: The Sound Which Stars Make Rushing Through the Sky; aka Jane Johnston Schoolcraft; poet and interpreter of Ojibway myths; married to Indian Agent Henry Rowe Schoolcraft; 1800-1841. Ojibway notable.

Obashkaandagaang: (ntg) aka Washagamis Bay First Nation (Ontario)

Obegwadans: Chief of the Earth; 1837 t.s. Ojibway notable.

Obwagunn: Thunder Turn Back; 1828 t.s. Winnebago notable.

Oconomowoc: River of Lakes. WI p.n.

Oconto: Pike (or Pickerel) Place, or River of Plentiful Fish. WI p.n.

Ocundecun: Bouy; 1854 t.s. Ojibway notable.

Odahwe, or Adawe, preferred pronounciation of OTTAWA; most often translated as Traders, To Trade (or Barter), or Bartering Place; it may also mean To Sell (not trade; possible source is from Odauwuwau ininiwuk, meaning Bullrush People; self desig. Anishnabeg: Original People; part of the Three Fires Confederacy; Ottawa divisions, Kiskakon: Cut Tails, or Bear Clan; Nassauaketon: People of the Fork; Sable: Sandy Country People; Sinago: Squirrel Clan; Michigan, Oklahoma, Ontario tribe; IL, KS, MI, NWT, OH, OK, Ont., Que., WV p.n.

Odauwau-ininiwuk: Bullrush People; possible source of OTTAWA: most often translated as Traders, To Trade (or Barter), or Bartering Place; it may also mean To Sell (not trade); tribal sources state that Adawe or Odahwe is preferred pronounciation; self desig. Anishnabeg: Original People; part of the Three Fires Confederacy; Ottawa divisions, Kiskakon: Cut Tails, or Bear Clan; Nassauaketon: People of the Fork; Sable: Sandy Country People; Sinago: Squirrel Clan; Michigan, Oklahoma, Ontario tribe; IL, KS, MI, NWT, OH, OK, Ont., Que., WV p.n.

Odauwuhnshk: Bullrush River. Possible source for Ottawa River. ON p.n.

Odawa (pronounced Oh'dawa): To Trade, or Traders; preferred form of Ottawa; self desig. Anishnabek: Original People, or Those Who Intend To Do Well. Michigan Tribal People.

Ogeetub: Trader; 1863 t.s. Ojibway notable.

Ogemaga: Dandy; 1837 t.s. Ojibway notable.

Ogemaw: Chief. MI p.n.

Ogemawwaychewaib: Chief of the Mountain; 1863 t.s. Ojibway notable.

Ogenheratarihiens: Hot Ash; aka Garonhiague: Celestial, or In the Sky; c1646-1687. Mohawk notable.

Ogimauh-binaessih: Chief Little Bird; aka Wageezhegome: Who Is Like the Day; aka John Cameron; Mississagua 1764 -1828. Ojibway notable.

Ogimaus: Little Chief (ie, chief of subordinate authority); 1837 t.s. Ojibway notable.

Ogisna Kegido: Chief Speaker; 1837 t.s. Ojibway notable.

OHIO: most often translated as Beautiful River, Large River, Fair to Look Upon, or simply Beautiful; other sources claim that the word is only a prefix meaning White Caps (or simply White). The full word for the river should then be Ohio pek hanne: River Whitened By Froth; or Ohiophanne: River Full of White Caps, or Very White River; also a CO, IL, IN, KY, NY, PA, WV place name.

Ohtowa'kehson (ntg): aka Catherine Brant (third wife of Joseph Brant); Turtle Clan Mother; c1759 1837. Mohawk notable.

OJIBWAY: translated variously as Those Who Make Pictographs, Talk of the Robin, Great Medicine People, or Puckered Up. This "Puckered Up" reference is usually associated with either the form of their moccasin seam or their supposed practice of roasting their enemies until they are "puckerd up" (which seems a bit ludicrous and does not make linguistic nor historic sense); Chippewa is assumed to be a corruption of Ojibway and is used interchangeably, and in this form its meaning has been given as: Gathering Up Voice, Voice Gathered Up, or Puckered Voice; Chippewa is usually used in the U.S., Ojibway in Canada. The tribe is very extensive and is found in Manitoba, Michigan, Minnesota, Montana, North Dakota, Ontario, Saskatchewan, and Wisconsin. They are part of the Three Fires Confederacy (with the Ottawa and Potawatomi); Ojibway used as place name in MI, MN, MT, WA. WI; the Sioux called them the Hahatonwan: the Camp at Falls People (a reference to Sault Ste. Marie).

Ojibways of Garden River: First Nation of Ontario

Ojibways of Onigaming: The Portage; First Nation of Ontario

Ojibways of Sucker Creek: First Nation of Ontario

Ojibways of the Pic River: First Nation of Ontario

Ojiji Ziibi: source of Rainy River First Nation (Ontario)

Okakaning: Fishing Place, or Crow nesting Place, or Long Portage; source of Kaukauna. WI p.n.

Okemance: Young Chief, 1817 t.s. (see Ogimaus, above). Ojibway notable.

Okemas: Little Chief; 1815 t.s. Ottawa notable.

Okemos: Secondary Chief, or Little Chief. MI p.n.

Old Chief: Hoongkah; 1837 t.s. Winnebago notable.

Old Man: Awkewainze; 1854 t.s. Ojibway notable.

Old Woman Lake: Mindemoya (Lake). ON p.n.

On the River: Washtenaw, or Far Off. MI p.n.

On the Rock, or Green Lake: Gogebic. WI p.n.

Onanquatgo: Big Medicine; aka Norbert S. Hill, Jr.; educator; author; 1946 . Oneida notable.

Onaping: from Onumananing: Red Paint, or Vermillion. ON p.n.

Onayotekaono (Granite People): Oneida. or Ratirontakowa (People of the Big Log).

One Horn: Hazhunkeetaw; 1855 t.s. Winnebago notable.

One Standing Ahead: Nawgawnegawbow; 1863 t.s. Ojibway notable.

One Stops Talking To Another: Ponemah. MN p.n.

One that Stands And Reaches the Sky: Mawhecooshawnawzhekaw; aka Little Decora; 1797-1887; 1855 t.s. Winnebago notable.

One Who Carries the Voice: Myyawgewaywedunk; 1854 t.s. Ojibway notable.

One Who Is Exalted: Kezhogowinninne; or Skyman, or Man of the Sky; Mississauga; 1812 1889. Ojibway notable.

One Who Is Talked About: Kanapima; aka Augustin Hammelin, Jr.; 1813 ?. Ottawa notable.

One Who Pulls Down the People, or His Body Is Taken Down from Hanging: Atiatoharongwen; aka Louis Cook; c1740 1814. Mohawk notable.

One Who Puts Things in Order, or She Hesitates: Tekakwitha; aka Kateri; Mohawk holy woman made a Catholic Saint in 2012; 1656-1680. WI p.n.

One Who Steps Over the Sky: Bauzhi-geezhig-waeshikum; Ojibway notable. ?-1841.

One Who Went in Front: Karbenequane; 1815 t.s. Ottawa notable.

Oneida Nation of the Thames; First Nation of Ontario

ONEIDA: from Onuyo'teaka': People of the Standing (or Upright) Stone, or Stone People; or from Onayotekäono: Granite People; aka Ratirontakowa: People of the Big Log; New York, Ontario, Wisconsin tribe; part of the Iroquois Conf.; NY, ON, TN, WI p.n.

Ongwaterohiathe: He Lightens the Sky for Us; aka Swateny (from Onkhiswathetani: Our Enlightener); ?-1748. Oneida notable.

Onion, or Garlic, or Leek: Chicacwa; possible source of Chicago; WI p.n.

Onion: Chicago --possibly from Chicacwa: Garlic, Onion, Leek, Onion Place, or Garlic Field. IL p.n.

Onitariio: Beautiful Lake; possible source of Ontario; or from Kanadario: Sparkling Water; or from Ontarack: Rocks Standing High in the Water; other possible meanings: Great Lake, Beautiful Lake, Handsome Lake, or Large Lake; NY, OR, WI p.n.

ONONDAGA, from Onundägaono: People on (Top of) the Hills, or from Onontakehaka: People of the Hill; aka Hodiseññageta: Name Bearers; New York, Ontario tribe; part of the Iroquois Confederacy; NY p.n.

Onontakehaka (People on the Hills): Onondaga. or Onundägaono (People of the Hill).

Ononwarogo: Red Head; ?-1764. Onondaga notable

Onqueess: Mink; 1825 t.s. Ojibway notable.

Onqunogesh: Ugly Fellow; 1815 t.s. Ottawa notable.

Ontarack: Rocks Standing High in the Water; possible source of Ontario; or from Kanadario: Sparkling Water; or from Onitariio: Beautiful Lake; other possible meanings: Great Lake, Beautiful Lake, Handsome Lake, or Large Lake; NY, OR, WI p.n.

ONTARIO, several possible meanings: from Kanadario: Sparkling Water; or from Onitariio: Beautiful Lake; or from Ontarack: Rocks Standing High in the Water; other possible meanings: Great Lake, Beautiful Lake, Handsome Lake, or Large Lake; NY, OR, WI p.n.

Ontonagon: Place Where Game Was Shot By Luck. MI p.n.

Onumananing: Red Paint, or Vermillion; possible source of Wunnumin: Lake of Beaver Meal Fragments. Ontario First Nation.

Onundägaono: People on (Top of) the Hills, or from Onontakehaka: People of the Hill; the ONONDAGA; aka Hodiseññageta: Name Bearers; New York, Ontario tribe; part of the Iroquois Confederacy; NY p.n.

Onuyo'teaka': People of the Standing Stone; the Oneida. Ontario Tribe/First Nation.

Onwanonsyshon (ntg): aka George Henry Martin Johnson; Six Nations chief; 1816 1884. Mohawk notable.

Onwarenhiiaki: Tree Cutter; aka Williams, Eleazar; claimed to be the Lost Dauphin of France; controversial preacher; 1788-1858. Mohawk notable.

Oozawekwun: Yellow Quill. (one Canadian treaty [CDN 124], signed in 1871, listed the signers as "Ojibway/Cree").

Open Mouth: Tuscarawas. OH p.n.

Open Voice, or Through the Opening: Deyotha'gwende: aka Gawehe (ntg); ?-1766. Oneida notable.

Opening in the Sky, or Hole in the Day: from: Bugonegijig; 1825-1868. Ojibway notable.

Opening, or Bay in the Lake: Kanitareonto; possible source of Toronto: Fallen Trees in the Water, or Meeting Place; or from Deondo: Trees Growing Out of the Water; or from Thorontohen: Timbers on the Water. ON p.n.

Opeongo: Sandy at the Narrows. ON p.n.

Original Beings: Ukwehu:we; Oneida word used to refer to the continent's original inhabitants.

Original People: Anishinabek, or Those Who Intend To Do Well; self designation of the Ojibway (Chippewa), Ottawa, and Potawatomi. Great Lakes Tribal People.

Oronhyatekha: Burning Cloud; aka Peter Martin; physician, author; 1841-1907. Mohawk notable.

Osaukieuck: Yellow Earth People; source of Sauk. WI p.n.

Oscaquassanu: Young Boy; 1805 t.s. Ojibway notable.

Oscawbaywis: Waiter; 1854 t.s. Ojibway notable.

Osceola: Black Drink Hallower; Seminole; c1803-1838. MI, PA, WI p.n.

Oscoda: Rocky Prairie. Most likely not of Native origin. MI p.n.

Oshawa: Carrying Place, To Go to the Other Side, or Stream Crossing. ON p.n.

Oshkosh: Hoof, Claw, Nail; Menominee; 1795-1858. WI p.n.

Oskenawway: Youth; 1854 t.s. Ojibway notable.

Osnaburgh: now known as Mishkeegogamang (ntg) First Nation (Ontario)

Oswego: Flowing Out (as a river into a lake), or Outpouring. IL, WI p.n.

Otreouti: Big Mouth; fl. 1659-1688. Onondaga notable.

Otsego: Place of the Rock. MI, WI p.n.

OTTAWA: most often translated as Traders, To Trade (or Barter), or Bartering Place; it may also mean To Sell (not trade); tribal sources state that Adawe or Odahwe is preferred; possible source is from Odauwau ininiwuk, meaning Bullrush People; self desig. Anishnabeg: Original People; part of the Three Fires Confederacy; Ottawa divisions, Kiskakon: Cut Tails, or Bear Clan; Nassauaketon: People of the Fork; Sable: Sandy Country People; Sinago: Squirrel Clan; Michigan, Oklahoma, Ontario tribe; IL, KS, MI, NWT, OH, OK, Ont., Que., WV p.n.

Ottawa River, possibly from Odauwuhnshk: Bullrush River. ON p.n.

Ottawaus: Little Ottawa; 1837 t.s. Ojibway notable.

Otter (etc.): Kalamazoo, of Native origin, with several possible translations: It Smokes, Smoke, or Otter's Water; or from Kekekalakalamazoo: Where the Water Boils (or Smokes) in the Pot; or from Negikanamazo: Otter Tail, Beautiful Water, Boiling Water, or Stones Like Otters; or from Kikalamozo: He Is Inconvienced By Smoke In His Lodge. MI p.n.

Otter: Negig; 1807 t.s. Ojibway notable.

Outagamie: Dwellers on the Other Side. WI p.n.

Outlet: Sangamon: Outlet, or Plenty to Eat Land. IL p.n.

Outoutagan (ntg): aka Jean Le Blanc; fl. 1698-1712. Ottawa notable.

Outpouring: Oswego. IL p.n.

Owasco: Floating Bridge. IN p.n.

Ozaukee: Mouth of the River, or Yellow Earth Place. WI p.n.

Ozhawwawscogezhick: Blue Sky; 1854 t.s. Ojibway notable.

- *P* -

Paanassee: Bird; 1815 t.s. Ojibway notable.

Paashineep: Man Shooting at the Mark; 1825 t.s. Ojibway notable.

Pagawewewetung: Coming Home Hollowing; 1837 t.s. Ojibway notable.

Pagoonakeezhig: Hole in the Day: 1837 t.s. Ojibway notable.

Pahtahsega: He Who Comes Shining, or One Who Makes the World Brighter; aka Peter Jones; Mississauga Ojibway, Methodist minister; c1807-1890. Ojibway notable.

Painted Rocks: Mazinaubikaung. MI p.n.

Painted Rocks: originally Mazinaubikaung. MI p.n.

Pamozet (ntg): aka Armstrong; 1805 t.s. Munsee notable.

Panther (or Cougar) Place: Erie; or (less likely) from Yenrash: It Is Long tailed, or Panther; NY, OH, ON, PA p.n.

Panther Crouching for Its Prey: Tecumseh. MI, ON p.n.

Papnescha: Turn Round About; 1815 t.s. Ojibway notable.

Pappellond: Beaver Hat; 1805 t.s. Munsee notable.

Paquaamo: Woodpecker; 1837 t.s. Ojibway notable.

Parry Island: former name for Wasauksing First Nation (Ontario): Place that Shines Brightly in the Reflection of the Sacred Light

Partridge: Alpena County given "Indian-sounding" name by Indian Agent Henry Rowe Schoolcraft, possibly meant to refer to the Partridge. MI p.n.

Pasequamjis: Commissioner; 1837 t.s. Ojibway notable.

Pashkayraykaw: Fire Holder; 1832 t.s. Winnebago notable.

Pashkoninitigong (originally): Cloquet; Barren Place. MN p.n.

Paskeshegay: Rushing Water, or Shooting Water; aka Kapuskasing; ON p.n.

Passabikang: Steep Cliff; original name for Red Cliff. WI reservation.

Passage Way: Sabaskong. ON p.n.

Passes Under Everything: Shoboshkunk; 1863, 1855 t.s. Ojibway notable.

Paxton Creek: from Pekstank: Creek with Pool. PA p.n.

Payajik: Lone Man; 1837 t.s. Ojibway notable.

Paybawmesay: Soarer; 1854 t.s. Ojibway notable.

Paymaubeemee: Him that Looks Over; 1828 t.s. Winnebago notable.

Pays Plat: (French) Flat Land; former name for Baagwaashiing First Nation (Ontario): Where the Water is Shallow

Peaceful Valley, Place of Entrance (or The Gate), Place Between Two Points, or At the Forks: Tioga: IL, PA p.n.

Peawanuck: Flintstone; new name for Winisk. ON p.n.

Pechegabua: aka Sawanabenase: Southern Bird; aka Grand Blanc; 1807 t.s. Ojibway notable.

Pedudence: Rat's Liver; 1863 t.s. (or Petuddunce). Ojibway notable.

Peechananim: Striped Feather; 1825 t.s. Ojibway notable.

Peemeecheekag: Porcupine Standing Sideways; ?-1891. Ojibway notable.

Peeseeker: Buffalo; 1825 t.s. Ojibway notable.

Peetwaweetam: Coming Voice; 1837 t.s. Ojibway notable.

Pejike: Buffalo; 1847 t.s. (see Pezheke, below). Ojibway notable.

Pekstank: Creek with Pool; source of Paxton Creek. PA p.n.

Pelican: Shaata; 1825 t.s. Ojibway notable.

Peltier, Leonard; aka Gwartheelass: He Leads the People; Ojibway Lakota activist, political pris-oner; 1944 Ojibway notable.

Pembina: from Anibiminani Zibi Wininiwug: High-bush Cranberry River People. Ojibway band.

Peneshaw: Eagle; 1818 t.s. Ottawa notable.

Penetanguishene: Place of White Falling Sands, or Where the Sand Slides Down the Bank. ON p.n.

Peninsula Dwellers (a reference to the Door Peninsula, WI): Miami. WI tribe.

Peninsula Dwellers: Wyandotte, or Islanders. MI, OH p.n.

Peninsula People, from Oumaumeg: Miami. or from Wemiamik: All Friends. IN, OH p.n.

Pennefeather, William: aka Kakekapenais: Bird Forever; (one Canadian treaty [CDN 124], signed in 1871, listed the signers as "Ojibway/Cree").

Pensweguesic: Jaybird; 1817 t.s. Ojibway notable.

People –Illinois, from Illini: Man; plural, Illiniwok: People, or Perfect and Accomplished Men; Illinois divisions: Cahokia (ntg), and Tamaroa: He Has a Cut Tail; Oklahoma tribe

People of the First Voice (or Big Voice): Ho-chunk Nation; the official name for the WINNEBAGO said to be from a Potawatomi word, Winpyeko, which means People of the Dirty Water, in reference to Green Bay, Wisconsin, their traditional homeland; also said to mean Fish Eaters, or People of the Sea; self designations said to be Hochunkgra: People of the Big Voice, Hutcangara: Big Fish People, or Hochagra: People of the Parent Speech; the Wisconsin tribe has officially changed its name to; Nebraska, Wisconsin tribe; IL, MN, NE, WI p.n.

People of the Longhouse: Haudenosaunee; aka Iroquois: from Algonquin Irinakhoiw: Rattle-snakes; Ontario Tribe/First Nation.

People of the Peninsula: Maumee. OH p.n.

People of the Place of the Fire, or Keepers of the Sacred Fire, or Fire Nation: Potawatomi; responsible for the Three Fires Confederacy Council Fire.

People of the Sea, or Fish Eaters: possible meanings of WINNEBAGO; said to be from a Potawatomi word, Winpyeko, which means People of the Dirty Water, in reference to Green Bay, Wisconsin, their traditional homeland; self designations said to be Hochunkgra: People of the Big Voice, Hutcangara: Big Fish People, or Hochagra: People of the Parent Speech; the Wisconsin tribe has officially changed its name to Ho chunk Nation: People of the First Voice; Nebraska, Wisconsin tribe; IL, MN, NE, WI p.n.

People of the Standing (or Upright) Stone, or Stone People: the Oneida: from Onuyo'teaka', or from Onayotekäono: Granite People; aka Ratirontakowa: People of the Big Log; New York, Ontario, Wisconsin tribe; part of the Iroquois Conf.; NY, TN, WI p.n.

People of the Stoney Country: Munsee (a Delaware sub tribe). PA tribe.

People of the Waters that Are Never Still (a reference to the Hudson River): Muhheconneok; aka Mahican: Wolf. WI tribe.

People on (Top of) the Hills, or from Onontakehaka: People of the Hill: from Onundägaono; the ONONDAGA; aka Hodiseññageta: Name Bearers; New York, Ontario tribe; part of the Iroquois Confederacy; NY p.n.

People Who Are the Standard by Which All Other People Are Measured: Lenni Lenapé. WI tribe.

People who Live on the Peninsula: Miami. or from Meahme (or Wemiamik): All Friends; aka the Pahkah Miami: Beautiful Miami; self desig. Twightwee, or Twatwa: Cry of the Crane. Indiana tribe.

People Without Moccasins: Chippawa [sic]. ON p.n.

Peoria: from Piwarea; He Comes Carrying a Pack on His Back, or simply, Carriers. IL, OH p.n.

Perfect Men --Illinois, from Illini: Man; plural, Illiniwok: People, or Perfect and Accom-plished Men; Illinois divisions: Cahokia (ntg), and Tamaroa: He Has a Cut Tail; Oklahoma tribe.

Perfect People, or Innu People: Neenoilno; self. desig. of the Montagnais: Mountaineers (French). Ontario Tribe/First Nation.

Peshawbestown: Odawa Reservation in northern Michigan; named after local Chief.

Peshawkay: Young Ox; 1795 t.s. Ojibway notable.

Peshekata: Marked Legs; 1818 t.s. Ottawa notable.

Peshtigo: Snapping Turtle, or Wild Goose. WI p.n.

Petawawa: Noise of Water Far Away is Heard. ON p.n.

Peter Jones; Kahkewaquonaby: Sacred Feathers; writer and Methodist minister; 1802 1856. Miss-issauga notable.

Peters, Hendrick; aka Theyanoguin: White Head; aka King Hendrick; sachem, diplomat; c1680-1755. Mohawk notable.

Peterson, Paulus; aka Sahonwagy: One On His Boat; educator, sachem; ?-1787. Mohawk notable.

Petuddunce: Rat's Liver; 1855 t.s. (see Pedudence). Ojibway notable.

Pewabik: Iron. WI p.n.

Peytshunkaw: Crane; 1829 t.s. Winnebago notable.

Pezheke: Buffalo; 1837 t.s. (see Pejike, above). Ojibway notable.

Pezhekins: Young Buffalo; 1837 t.s. Ojibway notable.

Pezhihutazizi Kapi (from): Yellow Medicine; Diggings of Yellow Plant Root (Moonseed). MN p.n.

Philadelphia; orig. Kuweukwanaku: Tall Pine Grove. PA p.n.

Piagick: Single Man; 1825 t.s. Ojibway notable.

Pic Mobert: now known as Netmizaaggamig Nishnaabeg (ntg) First Nation (Ontario)

Pickaway: Ashes Men (ie, they rose from ashes) . OH p.n.

Pickerel, or Pike: Kenosha. WI p.n.

Pictographs, Those Who Make: Ojibway; also translated as Talk of the Robin, or Puckered Up. This "Puckered Up" reference is usually associated with either the form of their moccasin seam or their supposed practice of roasting their enemies until they are "puckered up" (which seems a bit ludicrous and does not make linguistic nor historic sense); Chippewa is assumed to be a corruption of Ojibway and is used interchangeably, and in this form its meaning has been given as: Gathering Up Voice, Voice Gathered Up, or Puckered Voice; Chippewa is usually used in the U.S., Ojibway in Canada; The tribe is very extensive and is found in Manitoba, Michigan, Minnesota, Montana, North Dakota, Ontario, Saskatchewan, and Wisconsin. They are part of the Three Fires Confederacy (with the Ottawa and Potawatomi); Ojibway used as place name in MI, MN, MT, WA; the Sioux called them the Hahatonwan: the Camp at Falls People (a reference to Sault Ste. Marie)

Pictured Water: Missanabie Cree First Nation (Ontario)

Pictures on the Water (reference to pictographs along banks): Missinaibi. ON p.n.

Pierce, Jaris; aka Jahdahdieh: Sailing Whale; 19th c. clerk of the Six Nations. Onondaga notable.

Pikangikum: Lake of Calm Waters; First Nation of Ontario

Pike (or Pickerel) Place, or River of Plentiful Fish: Oconto. WI p.n.

Pike Kinongé: aka Le Brochet (Pike); fl. 1660-1713. Ottawa notable.

Pike Place: Ginozhaekaunning. Original name for Bay Mills. Michigan reservation.

Pike, or Pickerel: Kenosha. WI p.n.

Pinconning: Potato Place. MI p.n.

Pioneer: Negaunee: He Walks Ahead (ie. the Pioneer). MI p.n.

Pipe: Cheboygan (or Funnel). or from Shabwawagoning: Rumbling Waters, or Waters Disappearing Underground. MI p.n.

Pishkagaghe: White Crow; 1837 t.s. Ojibway notable.

Pittsburgh; orig. Menachksink: Where There Is a Fort. PA p.n.

Piwarea: Peoria. He Comes Carrying a Pack on His Back, or simply, Carriers. IL p.n.

Place Between Two Points, or Peaceful Valley, or Place of Entrance (or The Gate), or At the Forks: Tioga. PA p.n.

Place of Pines: Shingwauk. ON p.n.

Place of the Fire (People of the): Potawatomi. or Keepers of the Sacred Fire, or Fire Nation; responsible for the Three Fires Confederacy council fire; self desig. Anishnabek: Original People, or Those Who Intend To Do Well (see Potawatomi). Michigan Tribe.

Place of the Head: Wihling; source of Wheeling Creek. PA p.n.

Place of the Rapids, or River Beaten to a Spray: Baweting; original name for Sault Ste. Marie; MI p.n. ON p.n.

Place of the Red Earth People, Where the Waters Gather, or Red Stone: Meskousing; possible source of Wisconsin: with possible meanings: Muskrat Land, Grassy Place; or from Misconsin: Strong Current; or from Weeskonsan: Gathering of the Waters.

Place of the Rock: Otsego. WI p.n.

Place of the Sacs: Saginaw. Michigan reservation.

Place of the War God: Mexico (from the Aztec). OH, PA p.n.

Place of White Falling Sands, or Where the Sand Slides Down the Bank: Penetanguishene. ON p.n.

Place Where Alders Grow: Etobicoke; or from Wahdobekaung; Forest of Alders. ON p.n

Place Where Game Was Shot By Luck: Ontonagon: MI p.n.

Place Where the Dead Lie: Komoka. ON p.n.

Place Where the Waters Collect: Aumidjiwunaung: original name for Sarnia. ON p.n.

Place Where the Waters Flow Back and Forth: Waibejewung; aka Little Current. ON p.n.

Place Where Water is Shaped Like a Tooth: Wahnapitae First Nation (Ontario)

Plenty of Elk: Mooseomone; 1825 t.s. Ojibway notable.

Plenty to Eat Land. Sangamon: Outlet, or Plenty to Eat Land. IL p.n.

Plover (or Lapwing) Land: Moningwonaekauning; original name for La Pointe. WI p.n.

Plover: Chowwalksaihenic; 1837 t.s. Winnebago notable.

Pocohontas: Little Frolic. PA p.n.

Pocono: Valley Stream. PA p.n.

Pohopoko: Two Mountains with Stream Between; source of Poconos. PA p.n.

Point of Land: Neyashewun; source of Thessalon First Nation (Ontario)

Ponemah: One Stops Talking To Another. MN p.n.

Pontiac: from Bwondiac: Stopping It (in reference to his warning of an Iroquois raid which saved his village); or Stops By Use of A Stick; war chief; 1720-1769. Ottawa notable.

Poplar Hill: First Nation of Ontario

Poplar Point: First Nation of Ontario

Poquaquet: the Ball; 1807 t.s. Ojibway notable.

Porcupine Standing Sideways: Peemeecheekag; ? 1891. Ojibway notable.

Portage: Keweenaw. or Cross A Point. MI p.n.

Portage: Ojibways of Onigaming First Nation of Ontario

Poshquaygin: Leather; 1854 t.s. Ojibway notable.

Potato Place: Pinconning. MI p.n.

Potato Place: Topeka: Good Potato Place (from the Shawnee word for Jerusalem Artichoke). IL, IN p.n.

Potato: Macoupin. IL p.n.

Potawatomi: Keepers of the Sacred Fire. or People of the Place of the Fire, or Fire Nation; responsible for the Three Fires Confederacy council fire. Self desig. Anishnabek: Original People, or Those Who Intend To Do Well. Ontario Tribe/First Nation, Michigan Tribe, Wisconsin Tribe.

Potomac: Where Goods Are Brought In. IL p.n.

Powassan: Big Bend. ON p.n.

Powless, Henry: aka Wastheelgo; Throwing Up Pins; 19th c. Oneida notable.

Prairie du Chien: named after Fox chief known as Dog. WI p.n.

Prairie Hen, or To Cross a Point, or Wild Duck: Kewaunee; or from Kakiweonan: Land Crossing By Boat. WI p.n.

Prince, Henry; aka Miskookenew: Red Eagle; (one Canadian treaty [CDN 124], signed in 1871, listed the signers as "Ojibway/Cree").

Projecting Rock: Tyunayate; source of Juniata. PA p.n.

Provoker: Sagonehguahdeh; aka Albert Cusick; 19th c. Onondaga notable.

Puckenese: Spark of Fire; 1807 t.s. Ojibway notable.

Puckered Voice, or Voice Gathered Up: Chippewa: (see p.56 for complete discussion). WI p.n.

Pugaagik: Little Beef; 1825 t.s. Ojibway notable.

Puinanegi: Hole in the Day; 1825 t.s. Ojibway notable.

Pujikut: Bay in Spite of Everything; original name for Green Bay. WI p.n.

Punxsutawney: Gnat Place, or Sand fly Town. PA p.n.

Pure Water Source: Sandusky, or At the Cold Water. OH p.n.

Pure Water, or Cool Water: Sandusky. WI p.n.

Pure White: Wabash. or Bog River, or White Water, (in reference to its limestone bed) . IN p.n.

Pusisaingegen: Broken Arm; 1825 t.s. Ojibway notable.

- Q -

Quewezance: Hole in the Day; 1854, 1864, 1867 t.s.; also translated as: The Boy; 1864 t.s.; and White Fish; 1854 t.s. Ojibway notable.

Quick Heart: Nautchkaysuck; 1829, 1837 t.s. Winnebago notable.

Quietly: Topinabee: He Who Sits Quietly; notable 19th c. Potawatomi chief who signed many treaties. MI p.n.

Quinnesec Falls: Where It Is Noisy, or Smoke (in reference to mist from falls). WI p.n.

Quinnesec: from Pekwenesseg: Where the River Forms A Spray. MI p.n.

Quitchonequit: Big Cloud; 1805, 1807 t.s. Ojibway notable.

Quiweshenshish: Bad Boy; 1863 t.s. Ojibway notable.

- *R* -

Racoon: Geauga. OH p.n.

Raining Wind: Kemewenaush; 1863 t.s. Ojibway notable.

Rainy Lake: Koochiching. MN p.n.

Rainy River: Ojiji Ziibi; First Nation of Ontario

Rama First Nation: (Ontario) preferred designation is Chippewas of Mnjikaning: At the Fish Fence at the Narrows.

Rat's Liver: Washaskkokone; 1837 t.s. Ojibway notable.

Rat's Liver: Pedudence (or Petuddunce). 1863, 1855 t.s. Ojibway notable.

Ratirontakowa: People of the Big Log; the Oneida: from Onuyo'teaka': People of the Standing (or Upright) Stone, or Stone People; or from Onayotekäono: Granite People; New York, Ontario, Wisconsin tribe; part of the Iroquois Conf.; NY, TN, WI p.n.

.Rattle Snake: Waukaumkaw; 1829 t.s. Winnebago notable.

Rattlesnakes: IROQUOIS possibly from the Algonquin, Irinakhoiw, meaning Rattlesnakes, or Real Adders.

Raven Feather: Crow Wing: from Kagiwigwan: Crow (or Raven's) Wing, or Raven Feather. MN p.n.

Real Adders: IROQUOIS possibly from the Algonquin, Irinakhoiw, meaning Rattlesnakes, or Real Adders.

Real People: MOHAWK most often translated as Man-eaters, or Cannibals; possibly from Mohowauuck: They Eat Animate Things; also translated as Keepers of the Eastern Door. several self designations; Ongwe howe: Real People, Cannieigas: Flint People, Kanien'kéhaka: People of the Flint, and Gäneagaono: Possessors of the Flint; New York, Ontario, Quebec tribe (the Akwesasne Mohawk are of New York); part of the Iroquois confederacy; all of Mohawk territory is called Kanienkeh: Land of the Flint.

Real People, or Men of Our Nation: Lenape. PA p.n.

Rechouwhacky: Sandy Land; source of Rockaway. WI p.n.

Red Bear: Miscomukquah; 1863, 1864 t.s. Ojibway notable.

Red Bird: Miscopenenshay; 1863 t.s. Ojibway notable.

Red Bird: Wanig Suchka; 1788-1828. Winnebago notable.

Red Cliff; orig. Passabikang: Steep Cliff. WI reservation.

Red Eagle: Miskookenew; aka Henry Prince. (one Canadian treaty [CDN 124], signed in 1871, listed the signers as "Ojibway/Cree").

Red Earth: Muskoka. ON p.n.

Red Head: Cachointioni; ?-1756. Onondaga notable.

Red Head: Ononwarogo; ?-1764. Onondaga notable.

Red Lake: from Miskwagamiwi-sagaigun: Red-watered Lake. Minnesota reservation.

Red Leaf, or Red Battle Standard: Wabasha. MN p.n.

Red Paint, or Vermillion: Onumananing; possible source of Wunnumin: Lake of Beaver Meal Fragments. Ontario First Nation.

Red Paint, or Vermillion: Onumananing; source of Onaping. ON p.n.

Red River: Manistee (and Manistique). or Crooked River, or Wind Sound, or Lost River, or Wood's Spirit. MI p.n.

Red Rob: Miscoconoya; 1863 t.s. Ojibway notable.

Red Rock Band: First Nation of Ontario

Red Stone, or Place of the Red Earth People, Where the Waters Gather: Meskousing; possible source of Wisconsin: with possible meanings: Muskrat Land, Grassy Place; or from Misconsin: Strong Current; or from Weeskonsan: Gathering of the Waters.

Red War Eagle: Heetshahwaushaipsootskau; 1829 t.s. Winnebago notable.

Red Wing: Ahooshushkah; 1837 t.s. Winnebago notable.

Red Wing: from Koopoohoosha: Wing of the Wild Swan Dyed Scarlet. MN p.n.

Reed (Place of the): Munuscong. MI p.n.

Reed-Like, Needle, Awl, Disappearing River, Noise Underground, Thundering Under the Ground, or Something that Pierces: Sheboygan; or from Shabwawagoning: Rumbling Waters, or Waters Disappearing Underground. WI p.n.

Reflection of Sky on Water; Minnesota, with several other translations: Cloudy, Sky colored, Whitish, or Milky Water; Water Reflecting Cloudy Skies, or Land of Many Lakes.

Resounding with Great Noise, Bisected Bottom Lands, Neck of Land Between Lakes, or Thunder of Waters: Niagara; aka Kitchi Gaugeedjiwunng: Great Falls. ON p.n.

Returning Echo: Awawbedwaywedung; 1863 t.s. Ojibway notable.

Returning Sky: Keewaygeeshig; 1836 t.s. Ojibway notable.

Rice Maker: Munominekayshein (or Menomineekeshen); 1855, 1863 t.s. Ojibway notable.

Rich Land, or Good Earth: Mene-awkee; aka Milwaukee; or from Mino-aki: Fair, Fertile Land. WI p.n.

Ripple: Sinageewen; 1828 t.s. Winnebago notable.

River Beaten to a Spray, or Place of the Rapids: Baweting; original name for Sault Ste. Marie. MI p.n. ON p.n.

River Crossing Lake: Bemidji. MN p.n.

River Current Is Heard: Matachewan. Ontario First Nation.

River Digging Away Its Shores, or River with Sliding Banks: Monongahela; or from Menaun gehilla: River with Banks that Fall Down. PA p.n.

River Flowing Into the Lake, Where the Current Begins, or River Flowing Into Another Body of Water: Mattawa: ON p.n.

River Following the Line of the Lakeshore: Tittabawassee. MI p.n.

River Forms A Spray (Where the): Quinnesec: from Pekwenesseg: MI p.n.

River Having Many Outlets: Mississauga; an Ojibway subdivision, of Ontario. Newer documents group them as Ojibway. ON p.n.

River Junction, or Mouth of the River, or Lake Outlet: Mendota. MN, WI p.n.

River Maker: Hiawatha. MI p.n.

River of Lakes: Oconomowoc. WI p.n.

River of Many Mouths: Mississauga First Nation (Ontario)

River of Pines: Coaticook. ON p.n.

River of Plentiful Fish, or Pike (or Pickerel) Place: Oconto;. WI p.n.

River of Short Bends and Many Islands, or Always Plenty of Game: Kakabeka Falls. ON p.n.

River of the Lenape: Lenape Wihittuck; orig. name for the Delaware River; aka Maksrick kitton: Large River. PA p.n.

River That Twists About (from Azhaowesse): Shiawassee: Straight Ahead Water; MI p.n.

River Where Blue Earth Is Gathered: Makato River: from Makato-Osa-Watapa. MN p.n.

River with Banks that Fall Down: Menaun-gehilla; possible source of Monongahela: River Digging Away Its Shores, or River with Sliding Banks. PA p.n.

River: Yuma: Sons of the River. MI p.n.

Road Scraper: Johahgoehdeh; aka Daniel George; 19th c. Onondaga notable.

Roaring Thunder: Waukauntshawhayreekaw; 1832 t.s. Winnebago notable.

Robin, Talk of the: Ojibway; also translated as Those Who Make Pictographs, or Puckered Up. This "Puckered Up" reference is usually associated with either the form of their moccasin seam or their supposed practice of roasting their enemies until they are "puckered up" (which seems a bit ludicrous and does not make linguistic nor historic sense); Chippewa is assumed to be a corruption of Ojibway and is used interchangeably, and in this form its meaning has been given as: Gathering Up Voice, Voice Gathered Up, or Puckered Voice; Chippewa is usually used in the U.S., Ojibway in Canada; The tribe is very extensive and is found in Manitoba, Michigan, Minnesota, Montana, North Dakota, Ontario, Saskatchewan, and Wisconsin. They are part of the Three Fires Confederacy (with the Ottawa and Potawatomi); Ojibway used as place name in MI, MN, MT, WA; the Sioux called them the Hahatonwan: the Camp at Falls People (a reference to Sault Ste. Marie)

Rock (On the): Gogebic. or Green Lake, or High Lake, or Trembling Ground. MI p.n.

Rock (Place of the): Otsego. MI p.n.

Rock Bottom: Attawapiskat. ON p.n.

Rock Rising to a Point: Chattanooga. OH p.n.

Rockaway: from Rechouwhacky: Sandy Land. WI p.n.

Rocks in Deep Water, or Rocks Rising Out of River: Gananoque. ON p.n.

Rocks Standing High in the Water: Ontarack; possible source of Ontario; or from Kanadario: Sparkling Water; or from Onitariio: Beautiful Lake; other possible meanings: Great Lake, Beautiful Lake, Handsome Lake, or Large Lake; NY, OR, WI p.n.

Rocky Boy: aka Stone Child; 1860-1914. Ojibway notable.

Rocky Prairie: Oscoda. MI p.n.

Round Lake: Wauwi-autinoong. Original name for Lake St. Clair. MI, ON p.n.

Rumbling Waters, or Waters Disappearing Underground: Shabwawagoning; possible source of Sheboygan (WI p.n.) and Cheboygan (MI p.n.): Needle, Awl, Disappearing River, Noise Under-ground, Reed Like, Thundering Under the Ground, or Something that Pierces.

Running Water: Neenah. WI p.n.

Rushing Water, or Shooting Water: Paskeshegay; aka Kapuskasing. ON p.n.

- S -

Sabaskong: Passage Way. ON p.n.

Sable: Sandy Country People; People of the Fork: Nassauaketon; Kiskakon: Cut Tails, or Bear Clan; Sinago: Squirrel Clan. Ottawa divisions.

Sac Tribe (Place of the): Saginaw. MI p.n.

Sachigo Lake: (ntg) First Nation of Ontario

Sacred Feathers: Kahkewaquonaby; Peter Jones; writer and Methodist minister; 1802-1856. Mississauga notable.

Sadekanakte (ntg): aka Adaquarande (ntg); 1640-1701. Onondaga notable.

Sagamok Anishnawbek: Two Points Joining; First Nation of Ontario

Sagatagun: Spunk; 1837 t.s. Ojibway notable.

Saginaw: Place of the Sac Tribe. MI p.n. Michigan Reservation.

Sagonehguahdeh: Provoker; aka Albert Cusick; 19th c. Onondaga notable.

Saguima: Medicine Man; fl. 1707-44. Ottawa notable.

Sagwadacamegishcang: Tries the Earth; 1866 t.s. Ojibway notable.

Sahhugaene (ntg): aka Button George; 1838 t.s. Oneida notable.

Sahonwagy: One On His Boat; aka Paulus Peterson; educator, sachem; ?-1787. Mohawk notable.

Sailing Whale: Jahdahdieh; aka Jaris Pierce; 19th c. clerk of the Six Nations. Onondaga notable.

Sakayengwaraton: He Has Made the Mist Disappear for Them, or Disappearing Knot; aka John Johnson; aka Smoke Johnson; Pinetree chief; 1792-1886. Mohawk notable.

Salamonie: Yellow Paint. IN p.n.

Salt Lick: Mahanoy. PA p.n., and Mahoning. OH p.n.

Sand Point; First Nation of Ontario

Sand-fly Town, or Gnat Place: Punxsutawney. PA p.n.

Sandusky: At the Cold Water, or Pure Water Source. OH, WI p.n.

Sandy at the Narrows: Opeongo. ON p.n.

Sandy Country People: Sable; Kiskakon: Cut Tails, or Bear Clan; Nassauaketon: People of the Fork; Sinago: Squirrel Clan. Ottawa divisions.

Sandy Lake: First Nation of Ontario

Sandy Land: Rechouwhacky; source of Rockaway. WI p.n.

Sandy Stream: Legauihanne; source of Lycoming; or from Legawing: At the Place of Sand. PA p.n.

Sangamon: Outlet, or Plenty to Eat Land. IL p.n.

Saratogo: Beaver Place. WI p.n.

Sarnia; orig.; Aumidjiwunaung: Place Where the Waters Collect. ON p.n.

Sarothanewana: Two Hide Together; aka White, Charles; 19th c. Wolf clan leader. Mohawk notable.

Sasagohcumickishcum: Makes the Ground Tremble; 1864 t.s. Ojibway notable.

Sasunnahgandeeh: Half Name, or Half Blood; aka Joshua Jones; 19th c. Oneida notable.

Saugatuck: Tidal Outlet. MI p.n.

Saugeen: Mouth of the River; Ojibway First Nation; Ontario p.n.

Saugeen: Zaagiing: At the Mouth of the River; First Nation of Ontario

Sauk: from Osaukie-uck: Yellow Earth People. IL, WI p.n.

Sault Ste. Marie; orig. Baweting: Gathering Place of the People, Place of the Rapids, or River Beaten to a Spray. MI, ON p.n.

Sawanabenase: Southern Bird; aka Pechegabua; aka Grand Blanc; 1807 t.s. Ojibway notable.

Sawwaughkeewau: He that Leaves the Yellow Track; 1828 t.s. Winnebago notable.

Sawyer, Joseph; aka Nawahjegezhegwabe: Sloping Sky; Ojibway Grand Chief; 1786-1863. Ojibway notable.

Schoolcraft, Jane Johnston; aka Obahbahm-wawagezhegoqua: The Sound Which Stars Make Rushing Through the Sky; poet and interpreter of Ojibway myths; married to Henry Rowe Schoolcraft; 1800-1841. Ojibway notable.

Schuylkill: Hidden River (perhaps a Dutch word and not Native at all); orig. Ganshowehanne: Roaring Stream, or Noisy Stream Flowing Over. PA p.n.

Scioto: Deer; OH, WV p.n.

Screamer: Haukkaykaw; 1832 t.s. Winnebago notable.

Scugog: Muddy Bottom, or Submerged Land. ON p.n.

Secondary Chief, or Little Chief: Okemos. MI p.n.

Seine River: First Nation of Ontario

Seneca: Nundawaono (Great Hill People). or Tsionontowanehaka (People of the Big Mountain). New York, Ontario Tribe/First Nation.

Serpent River: First Nation of Ontario

Several Against One, or She Who is Outnumbered: from Degonwadonti; aka Beth Brant; writer, poet; 1941-2015. Mohawk notable.

Shaata: Pelican; 1825 t.s. Ojibway notable.

Shabwawagoning: Rumbling Waters, or Waters Disappearing Underground; possible source of Sheboygan (WI p.n.), Cheboygan (MI p.n.): Needle, Awl, Disappearing River, Noise Under-ground, Reed Like, Thundering Under the Ground, or Something that Pierces.

Shagobai: Little Six; 1837 t.s. Ojibway notable.

Shahwundais: Sultry Heat; aka John Sunday; Mississauga c1795-1875. Ojibway notable.

Shakanak: Slippery Fish (eel). IN p.n.

Shallow Bed River (or Dark colored Water): Tahquamenon. MI p.n.

Shallow Waterbed, or Lake with Many Islands: Kasabonika. Ontario First Nation.

Shamanetoo: God Almighty; 1815 t.s. Ojibway notable.

Shamokin: Eel Place. PA p.n.

Shaonkskawkaw: White Dog; 1828 t.s. Winnebago notable.

Shaugauwaumekong: Long Narrow Strip of Land Running Into the Water; aka Chequamegon. WI p.n.

Shawaghezhig: Sounding Sky; 1837 t.s. Ojibway notable.

Shawanaga: Long Bay or Strait, or South Portage. ON p.n.

Shawanaga: South Portage, Long Bay, or Strait; First Nation of Ontario

Shawano: To the South. WI p.n.

Shawfauwick: Mink; 1825 t.s. Ottawa notable.

Shawgawnawsheence: Little Englishman; 1854 t.s. Ojibway notable.

Shawshawwanebase: Falcon; aka John Tanner; adopted, lived as Ojibway, narrated biography; c1780-1846? Ojibway notable.

She Hesitates: Tekakwitha (Kateri): or One Who Puts Things in Order; aka The Lily of the Mohawks; Mohawk spiritual woman made a Saint by the Roman Catholic church in 2012; 1656-1680. IL, WI p.n.

She Who is Outnumbered, or Several Against One: from Degonwadonti; aka Beth Brant; writer, poet; 1941-2015. Mohawk notable.

Sheboygan: Needle, Awl, Disappearing River, Noise Underground, Reed Like, Thundering Under the Ground, or Something that Pierces; or from Shabwawagoning: Rumbling

Waters, or Waters Disappearing Underground. WI p.n., or Great Noise. ON p.n. Michigan place name spelled Cheboygan.

Sheganack: Black Bird; 1817 t.s. Ojibway notable.

Sheguiandah: Bay of Gray Slate; First Nation of Ontario

Sheltering Place: Waukegan. or Trading Post. IL p.n.

Shenandoah: Very Great Plain, Spruce Stream, or Beautiful Daughter of the Stars. PA p.n.

Shenango: Beautiful One. PA p.n.

Sheshegwaning: (ntg) First Nation of Ontario

Shiawassee: Straight Ahead Water; or from Azhaowesse: River That Twists About. MI p.n.

Shikellamy; aka Ongwaterohiathe: He Lightens the Sky for Us; aka Swateny (from Onkhis-wathetani: Our Enlightener); ?-1748. Oneida notable.

Shinggobe: Spruce; 1837 t.s. Ojibway notable.

Shinggoope: Balsom; 1854 t.s. Ojibway notable.

Shinguax: Cedar (or Pine); 1817 t.s. Ojibway notable.

Shingwauk: Place of Pines. ON p.n.

Shining Water: Iosco, or Water of Light. MI p.n.

Shirt Wearing People, or Hemp Gatherers: Tuscarora. Ontario Tribe/First Nation.

Shoal Lake 39: now known as Iskutewizaagegan (ntg) First Nation (Ontario)

Shoal Lake: First Nation of Ontario

Shoanktshunksaipkau: Black Wolf; 1828, 1829 t.s. Winnebago notable.

Shoboshkunk: Passes Under Everything; 1863, 1855 t.s. Ojibway notable.

Shogonickah: Little Hill; 1837, 1855 t.s. Winnebago notable.

Shohehdonah: Large Feather; aka Thomas La Forte; 19th c. Methodist minister. Onondaga notable.

Shonea: Silver; 1837 t.s. Ojibway notable.

Shooghattykah: Big Gun; 1837 t.s. Winnebago notable.

Shooting Water, or Rushing Water: Paskeshegay; aka Kapuskasing. ON p.n.

Shot By Luck: Ontonagon. Place Where Game Was Shot By Luck. MI p.n.

Shwanabe: Muskrat; 1818 t.s. Ottawa notable.

Silver Water: Horicon. WI p.n.

Silver: Shonea; 1837 t.s. Ojibway notable.

Silverheels, Jay: aka Harold Smith; actor who long-played the role of Tonto; 1912-1980. Mohawk notable.

Silversmith, Noah: aka Dahguoadah (ntg); 1838 t.s. Onondaga notable.

Silversmith: Honnonegadoh; 1838 t.s. Oneida notable.

Sinageewen: Ripple; 1828 t.s. Winnebago notable.

Sinago: Squirrel Clan; Kiskakon: Cut Tails, or Bear Clan; Nassauaketon: People of the Fork; Sable: Sandy Country People; Ottawa divisions.

Single Man: Piagick; 1825 t.s. Ojibway notable.

Siotinonawentowane: People of the Big Pipe: aka Cayuga, or Gweugwehono (People at the Mucky Land). NY tribe.

Sioux: aka Dakota. Minnesota tribe.

Six Nations of the Grand River: First Nation of Ontario

Skahlohahdieh: Beyond the Sky; aka George George; 19th c. Oneida notable.

Skanawati: Beyond the Swamp; aka John Buck; 19th c. Onondaga keeper of the wampum. Onondaga notable.

Skenandoa: Deer; 1706-1816. Oneida notable.

Skokie: Marsh. IL p.n.

Sky colored: Minnesota, with several translations: Cloudy, Whitish, or Milky Water; Water Reflecting Cloudy Skies; Reflection of Sky on Water; or Land of Many Lakes.

Sky that Touches the Ground: Mejawkekeshick; 1863 t.s. Ojibway notable.

Sky: Neesidaysish; 1825 t.s. Ojibway notable.

Skyman: Kezhogowinninne: or Man of the Sky, or One Who Is Exalted; Mississauga; 1812-1889. Ojibway notable.

Slate Falls: First Nation of Ontario

Sleepy Eyes: Ishtakhaba; after the Sisseton Dakota leader of the late 1800s. MN p.n.

Slippery Fish (eel): Shakanak. IN p.n.

Sloping Sky: Nawahjegezhegwabe; aka Joseph Sawyer; Ojibway Grand Chief; 1786-1863. Ojibway notable.

Small Porcupine: Cagouse; 1847 t.s. Ojibway notable.

Small Stick of Wood: from Enneasnekauntaa: aka Angus White; 19th c. Snipe clan leader. Mohawk notable.

Small Stream: Tunkhannock. PA p.n.

Smith, Harold: aka Jay Silverheels; actor who long-played the role of Tonto; 1912-1980. Mohawk notable.

Smoke (etc.): Kalamazoo, of Native origin, with several possible translations: It Smokes, Smoke, or Otter's Water; or from Kekekalakalamazoo: Where the Water Boils (or Smokes) in the Pot; or from Negikanamazo: Otter Tail, Beautiful Water, Boiling Water, or Stones Like Otters; or from Kikalamozo: He Is Inconvienced By Smoke In His Lodge. MI p.n.

Smoke (in reference to mist from falls), or Where It Is Noisy: Quinnesec Falls. WI p.n.

Smoke Johnson; aka John Johnson; aka Sakayengwaraton: He Has Made the Mist Disappear for Them, or Disappearing Knot; Pinetree chief; 1792-1886. Mohawk notable.

Smoker: Tshayrotshoankaw; 1828 t.s. Winnebago notable.

Snake Skin: Waukaunhahkaw (or Wakaunhakah; 1837 t.s.); 1828, 1829, 1832 t.s. Winnebago notable.

Snake: Kanabec. MN p.n.

Snake: Kaqueticum; 1868 t.s. (CDN 18). Ojibway notable.

Snake: Wakaunkah (or Waukaunkaw); 1828, 1832, 1837 t.s. Winnebago notable.

Snake's Skin: Wancahaga; 1825 t.s. Winnebago notable.

Snapping Turtle, or Wild Goose: Peshtigo. WI p.n.

Snow Crust: from Sosesaisnesakeken; aka Wood, Joseph; 19th c. Heron clan leader. Mohawk notable.

Snow, Joseph; aka Chanlyeya: Drifted Snow; 19th c. Onondaga notable.

So Long that You Cannot See the End of It: Nipigon; or from Animibeegoong: Along the Water's Edge, or Continuous Water. ON p.n.

Soarer: Paybawmesay; 1854 t.s. Ojibway notable.

Soil that is Rich, or Fertile: Waseca. MN p.n.

Soldier: Maunahpeykaw; 1832 t.s. Winnebago notable.

Solomon, Alexander; aka Archsisorihenn: He is to Blame; 19th c. leader. Mohawk notable.

Someone Lends Her a Flower: from Konwatsi'tsiaienni; aka Mary Brant; Clan Mother; c1736-1796. Mohawk notable.

Something that Pierces, Needle, Awl, Disappearing River, Noise Underground, Reed Like, Thundering Under the Ground: Sheboygan; or from Shabwawagoning: Rumbling Waters, or Waters Disappearing Underground. WI p.n. Michigan place name spelled Cheboygan).

Songakomig: Strong Ground; 1837 t.s. Ojibway notable.

Sons of the River: Yuma. MI p.n.

Sosesaisnesakeken: Snow Crust; aka Wood, Joseph; 19th c. Heron clan leader. Mohawk notable.

Sounding Sky: Shawaghezhig; 1837 t.s. Ojibway notable.

South (To the): Shawano. WI p.n.

Southern Bird: Sawanabenase; aka Pechegabua; aka Grand Blanc; 1807 t.s. Ojibway notable.

Sowengisik (ntg): Henry Bird Steinhauer; aka George Kachenooting (ntg); Ojibway educator; c1818-1884. Ojibway notable.

Spadina: from Ishapadenah: Hill (Toronto Street name). ON p.n.

Spaniard: Spanyoukaw; 1828 t.s. Winnebago notable.

Spanyoukaw: Spaniard; 1828 t.s. Winnebago notable.

Spark of Fire: Puckenese; 1807 t.s. Ojibway notable.

Sparkling Water: Kanadario: Ontario; possible source; or from Onitariio: Beautiful Lake; or from Ontarack: Rocks Standing High in the Water; other possible meanings: Great Lake, Beautiful Lake, Handsome Lake, or Large Lake; NY, OR, WI p.n.

Sparrow: Kahaka (or Kakaquap); 1825, 1837 t.s. Ojibway notable.

Spearing Fish from the End of a Canoe: Algonquin; or Spearing Fish Place. ON p.n.

Spirit Land, or River of Bad Spirits: Manitowoc:. WI p.n.

Spirit of the Day: Manotokeshick; 1863 t.s. Ojibway

Spirit: Manitou. MI p.n.

Spotted Arm: Manahkeetshumpkaw; 1828 t.s. Winnebago notable.

Spotted Earth: Menkayraykan; 1828 t.s. Winnebago notable.

Spruce Stream, or Very Great Plain, or Beautiful Daughter of the Stars: Shenandoah. PA p.n.

Spruce: Shinggobe; 1837 t.s. Ojibway notable.

Spunk: Sagatagun; 1837 t.s. Ojibway notable.

Sq___: Derogatory designation (the equivalent of the "c-word" in English). Virtually eliminated as place names in both the US and Canada; unfortunately, still used for local place names (roads, lakes, streams, creeks, etc.)

Squirrel Clan: Sinago; Kiskakon: Cut Tails, or Bear Clan; Nassauaketon: People of the Fork; Sable: Sandy Country People. Ottawa divisions.

Squirrel: Ojibway word is Chipmunk. WI p.n.

St. Clair, Lake; orig. Wauwi-autinoong: Round Lake. ON p.n.

St. Regis Reservation; aka Akwesasne: Land Where the Partridge Drums. Ontario First Nation.

Standard By Which All Men Are Measured: Lenni Lenape. Ontario Tribe/First Nation.

Standing Tree: from Hearenhodoh; aka Loft, John; 19th c. leader. Mohawk notable.

Stands Fast, Firm Standing, or He Who Stands Forever: from Kahgegagahbowh; aka George Copway; Mississauga Ojibway Methodist minister, writer; 1818-1869.

Stanjikoming: (a true misnomer) changing name to Mitaanjigamiing: Where Shallow Water Runs into Deep Water; First Nation of Ontario

Stayeghtha: He Causes It to Be Light for Us. Oneida notable.

Steep Cliff: Passabikang: source of Red Cliff. WI reservation.

Steinhauer, Henry Bird: aka George Kachenooting (ntg); aka Sowengisik (ntg); Ojibway educator; c1818-1884. Ojibway notable.

Stepping Ahead: Maugegawbow; 1855 t.s. Ojibway notable.

Stockbridge Munsee: an amalgamated tribe of Stockbridge people made up of Mahican and other Algonkian, and the Munsee who are a Delaware subgroup. Moved by the government to Wisconsin from the northeast in the 1840s. WI tribe.

Stone Child: aka Rocky Boy; 1860-1914. Ojibway notable.

Stone Country People: Muncie. IN p.n.

Stone Man: Eeneewonkshikkaw; 1832 t.s. Winnebago notable.

Stoney Country (People of the): Munsee; aka Muncie; Lenni Lenape sub tribe; Wisconsin tribe. The Stockbridge Munsee are an amalgamated tribe of Stockbridge people made up of Mahican, and other Algonkians, and the Munsee. Moved by the government to Wisconsin from the northeast in the 1840s.

Stony Country People: Munsee; aka Muncie. WI tribe.

Stopping It (in reference to his warning of an Iroquois raid which saved his village): Bwondiac; aka Pontiac; war chief; 1720-1769. Ottawa notable.

Stops By Use of A Stick: Pontiac. from Bonitiyak. MI p.n.

Straight Ahead Water: Shiawassee. or from Azhaowesse: River That Twists About. MI p.n.

Straight Bird: Tebeshcobeness; 1864 t.s. Ojibway notable.

Strait, Long Bay, or South Portage: Shawanaga First Nation (Ontario)

Stream Crossing, To Go to the Other Side, or Carrying Place: Oshawa. ON p.n.

Striped Feather: Peechananim; 1825 t.s. Ojibway notable.

Strong Current: Misconsin; possible source of Wisconsin: possible meanings: Muskrat Land, Grassy Place; or from Meskousing: Where the Waters Gather, Place of the Red Earth People, or Red Stone; or from; or from Weeskonsan: Gathering of the Waters.

Strong Ground: Songakomig; 1837 t.s. Ojibway notable.

Stumptail Bear: Aughquanahquose; 1814 t.s. Ottawa notable.

Sturgeon Place: Namekagon. WI p.n.

Sturgeon; Merrimac: Fish (sturgeon or catfish). WI p.n.

Stylish Person: Maisaninnine; aka Zhuawuno geezhigo gaubow: He Who Stands in the Southern Sky; aka; Jack Fiddler; c1830-1907. Ojibway notable.

Submerged Land, or Muddy Bottom: Scugog. ON p.n.

Subsistance Area: Dowagiac. MI p.n.

Sucre: Weescoup; 1825 t.s. Ojibway notable.

Sugar Maple: Wahta Mohawks First Nation (Ontario)

Sultry Heat: Shahwundais; aka John Sunday; Mississauga c1795-1875. Ojibway notable.

Summer Wolverine: Nebenequingwahawegaw; 1863 t.s. Ojibway notable.

Summer: Neebing. ON p.n.

Sunday, John; aka Shahwundais: Sultry Heat; Mississauga c1795-1875. Ojibway notable.

Superior, Lake; orig. Kitchi-gummeng: Great Lake (of the Ojibway). ON p.n.

Susquehanna: Muddy River; or from Guneshachachgak-hanne: Great Bend River. PA p.n.

Swamp People: Muskegon. or from Maskegowok: Swamp People. MI p.n.

Swamp River: Maski Sebi; original name for Bad River, from Masshki zeebi; ("maski" was mistook for "matchi," so we get Bad, not Swamp) . WI p.n.

Swamp: Muskigonce; 1868 t.s. (CDN 18). Ojibway notable.

Swampy (or Marshy River): Muskegon. or from Maskegowok: Swamp People. MI p.n.

Swampy Country: Kanakee. from Tehyakkeki: or Lowland. IN p.n.

Swampy or Marshy Land: Mississaugas of Scugog Island First Nation (Ontario)

Swan Creek Black River Confederated Ojibwa Tribes of Michigan: State-recognized Tribe of Michigan

Swateny (from Onkhiswathetani: Our Enlightener); aka Ongwaterohiathe: He Lightens the Sky for Us; ?-1748. Oneida notable.

Swift Current: Kashechewan. Ontario First Nation.

Swift Flying Hawk: Keshena. WI p.n.

Swiftly Flowing Waters: Magnetawan First Nation (Ontario)

- *T* -

Tahquamenon: Shallow Bed River, or Dark colored Water. MI p.n.

Takes the Leg of a Deer in His Mouth: Tshahsheerahwaukaw; 1832 t.s. Winnebago notable.

Tall Pine Grove: Kuweukwanaku; original name for Philadelphia. PA p.n.

Tamarack: from Hackmatack: Bad Lowlands (that is, the place where these trees grow). PA p.n.

Tanner, John; aka Shawshawwanebase: Falcon; adopted, lived as Ojibway, narrated biography; c1780-1846? Ojibway notable.

Tappan: Cold Stream. OH p.n.

Taquagana: Two Lodges Meeting; 1837 t.s. Ojibway notable.

Ta-ra-ke-te: Hat-rim Protects the Neck; aka Tarbell, Philip; 19th c. Wolf clan Mohawk chief. Mohawk notable.

Tarbell, Philip: Ta-ra-ke-te, Hat-rim Protects the Neck; 19th c. Wolf clan Mohawk chief. Mohawk notable.

Tarrier: Kiawatas; 1825 t.s. Ojibway notable.

Tashcuygon: (ntg) aka McArthur; 1815 t.s. Ottawa notable.

Taykwa Tagamou: (ntg) (formerly known as New Post First Nation); First Nation of Ontario

Tebeshcobeness: Straight Bird; 1864 t.s. Ojibway notable.

Tebishcogeshick: Equal Sky; 1864 t.s. Ojibway notable.

Tecumseh: Panther Crouching for Its Prey. MI, ON p.n.

Tedawkawmosay: Walking to And Fro; 1863 t.s. Ojibway notable.

Tehoragwanegen: He Has Placed Two Worlds Together; aka Thomas Williams; c1758-1849. Mo-hawk notable.

Tehowagherengaraghkwen (ntg): aka Thomas Davis; c1755 c1840. Mohawk notable.

Teiorhenhsere (ntg): aka Little Abraham; ?-1780. Mohawk notable.

Tekahionwake: Double Wampum; aka Johnson, Emily Pauline; writer, poet; 1861-1913. Mohawk notable.

Tekakwitha (Kateri): One Who Puts Things in Order, or She Hesitates; aka The Lily of the Mohawks; Mohawk spiritual woman made a Saint by the Roman Catholic church in 2012; 1656-1680. IL, WI p.n.

Tekarihogen (ntg): aka John Brant; youngest son of Joseph Brant; 1794-1832. Mohawk notable.

Tekawironte: Two Infants Stand Out; aka William Johnson; c1750-1777. Mohawk notable.

Temagami: Deep Water by the Shore; First Nation of Ontario

Teme-agama Anishnabay: aka Bear Island People. Ontario Tribe/First Nation.

Temiscaming: Deep Dry Water Place (dry in summer). ON p.n.

Teyemthohisa: Two Doors Closed; aka Isaac Hill; 19th c. Onondaga notable.

Teyoninhokerawen (ntg): aka Major John Norton; 1784-1825. Mohawk notable.

Thaunwankaw: Wild Cat; 1828 t.s. Winnebago notable.

Thayendanegea: He Places Together Two Bets; aka Joseph Brant, 1743?-1807. Mohawk notable. Source of Brantford, Ontario.

The Hook: Kiotseaeton: Mohawk notable.

The Light, White Cloud, or White Sky Light: Wabokieshek; aka The Winnebago Prophet; 1794-1841. Winnebago notable.

The One with the Silver Tongue: Minweweh; aka Minavavana; aka Le Grand Saulteur; c1710-1770. Ojibway notable.

The Sound Which Stars Make Rushing Through the Sky: Obahbahm-wawagezhegoqua; aka Jane Johnston Schoolcraft; poet and interpreter of Ojibway myths; married to Henry Rowe Schoolcraft; 1800-1841. Ojibway notable.

Thessalon: from Neyashewun: Point of Land; First Nation of Ontario

Theyanoguin: White Head; aka King Hendrick; aka Hendrick Peters; sachem, diplomat; c1680-1755. Mohawk notable.

Thoapnuzheekaw: Four Who Stand; 1829 t.s. Winnebago notable.

Thomas Bay (on Manitoulin Island); aka Wanoshkang Bay: You Must Go Around. ON p.n.

Thorontohen: Timbers on the Water: possible source of Toronto: Fallen Trees in the Water, or Meeting Place; or from Deondo: Trees Growing Out of the Water; or from Kanitareonto: Bay in the Lake, or Opening. ON p.n.

Those of the First Race: Iyiniwok; aka Cree; Cree is from the French, Kristinaux (ntg). Ontario Tribe/First Nation.

Those Who Intend To Do Well: Anishinabek, or Original People; self designation of the Ojibway (Chippewa), Ottawa, and Potawatomi. Great Lakes Tribal People.

Those Who Make Pictographs: Ojibiweg: possible source of Ojibway. Ontario Tribe/First Nation.

Three Channels: Nissodjiwunaung; aka Walpole Island (Unceded Indian Territory). Ontario First Nation.

Three Fires Confederacy council fire, responsible for the; Potawatomi: Fire Nation, or People of the Place of the Fire, or Keepers of the Sacred Fire; Ontario Tribe/First Nation.

Three Fires Confederacy member: Ottawa: most often translated as Traders, To Trade (or Barter), or Bartering Place; it may also mean To Sell (not trade); tribal sources state that Adawe or Odahwe is preferred pronunciation; possible source is from Odauwau ininiwuk, meaning Bullrush People; self desig. Anishnabeg: Original People; part of the; Ottawa divisions, Kiskakon: Cut Tails, or Bear Clan; Nassauaketon: People of the Fork; Sable: Sandy Country People; Sinago: Squirrel Clan; Michigan, Oklahoma, Ontario tribe; IL, KS, MI, NWT, OH, OK, Ont., Que., WV p.n.

Three Fires Confederacy: (one of the Tribes thereof). **Ojibway** translated variously as Those Who Make Pictographs, Talk of the Robin, or Puckered Up. This "Puckered Up" reference is usually associated with either the form of their moccasin seam or their supposed practice of roasting their enemies until they are "puckerd up" (which seems a bit ludicrous and does not make linguistic nor historic sense); Chippewa is assumed to be a corruption of Ojibway and is used interchangeably, and in this form its meaning has been given as: Gathering Up Voice, Voice Gathered Up, or Puckered Voice; Chippewa is usually used in the U.S., Ojibway in Canada; The tribe is very extensive and is found in Manitoba, Michigan, Minnesota, Montana, North Dakota, Ontario, Saskatchewan, and Wisconsin. They are part of the Three Fires Confederacy (with the Ottawa and Potawatomi); Ojibway used as place name in MI, MN, MT, WA; the Sioux called them the Hahatonwan: the Camp at Falls People (a reference to Sault Ste. Marie).

Through the Opening, or Open Voice: Deyotha'gwende; aka Gawehe (ntg); ?-1766. Oneida notable.

Thunder Bay: from the Native, Animikie Wekwed; orig. Gamanautigawaeyauk: Land of Many River Islands. ON p.n.

Thunder Mtn.: from Chequah Bikwaki. WI p.n.

Thunder of Waters, Bisected Bottom Lands, Neck of Land Between Lakes, or Resounding with Great Noise: Niagara; aka Kitchi Gaugeedjiwunng: Great Falls. ON p.n.

Thunder Sitting: Nunqueweebee; 1828 t.s. Winnebago notable.

Thunder Turn Back: Obwagunn; 1828 t.s. Winnebago notable.

Thundering Under the Ground, Needle, Awl, Disappearing River, Noise Underground, Reed Like, or Something that Pierces: Sheboygan; or from Shabwawagoning: Rumbling Waters, or Waters Disappearing Underground. WI p.n. Michigan place name spelled Cheboygan.

Tidal Outlet: Saugatuck. MI p.n.

Tide water: Nanticoke. ON, PA p.n.

Tieranensanoken: Deer House; aka Peter Herring, 19th c. Turtle Clan leader. Mohawk notable.

Timagami: Deep Water. ON p.n.

Timbers on the Water: Thorontohen; possible source of Toronto: Fallen Trees in the Water, or Meeting Place; or from Deondo: Trees Growing Out of the Water; or from Kanitareonto: Bay in the Lake, or Opening. ON p.n.

Timiskaming: Deep Water, or In the Deep Water. ON p.n.

Tioga: Peaceful Valley, Place of Entrance (or The Gate), Place Between Two Points, or At the Forks. IL, PA p.n.

Tippacanoe, or Tippecanoe: from Ketapekonnong: Buffalo Fish Place. IN, OH p.n.

Tittabawassee: River Following the Line of the Lakeshore. MI p.n.

To Cross a Point, Prairie Hen, or Wild Duck: Kewaunee; or from Kakiweonan: Land Crossing By Boat. WI p.n.

To Go to the Other Side, Stream Crossing, or Carrying Place: Oshawa. ON p.n.

To Sell (not trade): Ottawa; most often translated as Traders, To Trade (or Barter), or Bartering Place; tribal sources state that Adawe or Odahwe is preferred; possible source is from Odauwau ininiwuk, meaning Bullrush People; self desig. Anishnabeg: Original People; part of the Three Fires Confederacy; Ottawa divisions, Kiskakon: Cut Tails, or Bear Clan; Nassauaketon: People of the Fork; Sable: Sandy Country People; Sinago: Squirrel Clan; Michigan, Oklahoma, Ontario tribe; IL, KS, MI, NWT, OH, OK, Ont., Que., WV p.n.

Tomahawk: Wabawgamagau; 1866 t.s. Ojibway notable.

Tondagonee: Furious Dog; 1837 t.s. Ojibway notable.

Tondawganie (Toutogana, Tontegenah, or Tontagimi): Dog; 1805, 1815, 1817, 1818 t.s. Ottawa notable.

Tonto: Silverheels, Jay; aka Harold Smith; actor who long-played the role of Tonto; 1912-1980. Mohawk notable.

Tootagen: Bell; 1814 t.s. Ottawa notable.

Topeka: Good Potato Place (from the Shawnee word for Jerusalem Artichoke). IL, IN p.n.

Topinabee: He Who Sits Quietly; notable 19th c. Potawatomi chief who signed many treaties, under various spellings. MI p.n.

Toronto: Fallen Trees in the Water, or Meeting Place; or from Deondo: Trees Growing Out of the Water; or from Kanitareonto: Bay in the Lake, or Opening; or from Thorontohen: Timbers on the Water. ON p.n.

Toshunukhohonik (or Toshunuckah): Little Otter; 1832, 1837 t.s. Winnebago notable.

Towanda: Burial Place. IL, PA p.n.

Town on the Great River, or At the Big River: Kittanning. PA p.n.

Trade or Bartering Place: Ottawa; Basil Johnston, an Ojibway speaker, says the word means To Sell, not To Trade; he also says that the Ottawa River is named from Odauwuhnshk, which means Bullrush River. MI, ON p.n.

Trader: Ogeetub; 1863 t.s. Ojibway notable.

Traders, or To Trade: Odawa (pronounced Oh'dawa). preferred form of Ottawa; self designation: Anishnabek: Original People, or Those Who Intend To Do Well. Michigan Tribal People.

Traders, to Trade (or Barter): Ottawa; or Bartering Place; it may also mean To Sell (not trade); tribal sources state that Adawe or Odahwe is preferred; possible source is from Odauwau ininiwuk, meaning Bullrush People; self desig. Anishnabeg: Original People; part of the Three Fires Confederacy; Ottawa divisions, Kiskakon: Cut Tails, or Bear Clan; Nassauaketon: People of the Fork; Sable: Sandy Country People; Sinago: Squirrel Clan; Michigan, Oklahoma, Ontario tribe; IL, KS, MI, NWT, OH, OK, Ont., Que., WV p.n.

Trading Post: Waukegan. or Sheltering Place, IL p.n.

Travelling Sky: Mawjekeshick; 1863 t.s. Ojibway notable.

Tree Cutter: from Onwarenhiiaki; akaWilliams, Eleazar; claimed to be the Lost Dauphin of France; controversial preacher; 1788-1858. Mohawk notable.

Tree with Sweet Juice: Chanhassen. MN p.n.

Trees Growing Out of the Water: Deondo; possible source of Toronto: Fallen Trees in the Water, or Meeting Place; or from Kanitareonto: Bay in the Lake, or Opening; or from Thorontohen: Timbers on the Water. ON p.n.

Trembling Ground: Gogebic. or Green Lake, or High Lake, or On the Rock. MI p.n.

Tries the Earth: Sagwadacamegishcang; 1866 t.s. Ojibway notable.

Trout Lake: Namaygoosisagagun First Nation (Ontario) (non-Status)

Tshahsheerahwaukaw: Takes the Leg of a Deer in His Mouth; 1832 t.s. Winnebago notable.

Tshahtshunhatatykaw: Big Wave; 1832 t.s. Winnebago notable.

Tshayoskawtshokaw: He Who Plays with the Ox; 1829 t.s. Winnebago notable.

Tshayrotshoankaw: Smoker; 1828 t.s. Winnebago notable.

Tshuonuzheekau: He Who Stands in the House; aka Karraymaunee: Walking Turtle; 1829, 1832 t.s. Winnebago notable.

Tsionontowanehaka (People of the Big Mountain): Seneca. or Nundawaono (Great Hill People).

Tugonakeshik: Hole in the Day; 1855 t.s. Ojibway notable.

Tukaubishoo: Crouching Lynx; 1825 t.s. Ojibway notable.

Tunkhannock: Small Stream. PA p.n.

Turn Round About: Papnescha; 1815 t.s. Ojibway notable.

Turtle that Walks: Carimine; 1825 t.s. Winnebago notable.

Turtle: Mikinak; ?-1755. Ottawa notable.

Turtle: Misquadace; 1864 t.s. Ojibway notable.

Tuscarawas: Open Mouth. OH p.n.

Tuscarora: Shirt Wearing People, or Hemp Gatherers. Ontario Tribe/First Nation.

Tuscola: Warrior Prairie, or Level Lands. MI p.n.

Tushquagon (ntg): aka McCarty; 1805, 1818 t.s. (see Misquegin). Ottawa notable.

Twatwa: Miami. from Meahme (or Wemiamik): All Friends; aka the Pahkah Miami: or from Omaumeg: People who Live on the Peninsula; or Beautiful Miami; self desig. Twightwee, or Twatwa: Cry of the Crane. Indiana tribe:

Twelve O'clock: Nowgeshick; 1815 t.s. Ojibway notable.

Twightwee: Miami. from Meahme (or Wemiamik): All Friends; aka the Pahkah Miami: or from Omaumeg: People who Live on the Peninsula; or Beautiful Miami; self desig. Twightwee, or Twatwa: Cry of the Crane. Indiana tribe:

Twin-haired Bird: Adawawnequabenace. 1866 t.s. Ojibway notable.

Two Birds: Neesopena; 1825 t.s. Ojibway notable.

Two Doors Closed: Teyemthohisa; aka Isaac Hill; 19th c. Onondaga notable.

Two Hide Together: from Sarothanewana; aka White, Charles;; 19th c. Wolf clan leader. Mohawk notable.

Two Horns: Haynoampkaw; 1832 t.s. Winnebago notable.

Two Infants Stand Out: from Tekawironte: aka William Johnson; c1750-1777. Mohawk notable.

Two Lodges Meeting: Taquagana; 1837 t.s. Ojibway notable.

Two Mountains with Stream Between: Pohopoko; source of Poconos. PA p.n.

Two Points Joining: Sagamok Anishnawbek First Nation (Ontario)

Two Rivers Flowing Together: Dekanawida. Iroquois prophet and co founder (with Hiawatha) of the League of the Iroquois; 1550?-1600? Iroquois notable.

Tyunayate: Projecting Rock; source of Juniata. PA p.n.

- *U* -

Ugly Fellow: Onqunogesh; 1815 t.s. Ottawa notable.

Ukwehu:we: Original Beings; Oneida word used to refer to the continent's original inhabitants.

Unceded Indian Territory. Walpole Island; orig. Nissodjiwunaung: Three Channels. Ontario First Nation.

Unceded Indian Territory. Wikwemikong (Manitoulin Is.): Beaver Bay. Ontario First Nation.

Union of Waters: Coshocton, or Black Bear Town. OH p.n.

Upright Woman: Nahnebahwequay; Ojibway activist; 1824-1865.

- *V* -

Valley Stream: Pocono. PA p.n.

Venango: Figure Carved on a Tree. PA p.n.

Vermillion, or Red Paint: Onumananing; also possible source of Onaping; ON p.n.; also possible source of Wunnumin: Lake of Beaver Meal Fragments. Ontario First Nation.

Very Great Plain, Spruce Stream, or Beautiful Daughter of the Stars: Shenandoah. PA p.n.

Village: Chillicothe. IL p.n, OH p.n.

Village Enclosed by Stepped Cliffs: M'Chigeeng First Nation (Ontario)

Voice Gathered Up, or Puckered Voice: Chippewa (see Ojibway, p.102, for complete discussion).

- *W* -

Wabanaquot: White Cloud; 1830-1898. Ojibway notable.

Wabash: Bog River, Color-bright, or White Water. IL p.n.

Wabasha: Red Leaf, or Red Battle standard. MN p.n.

Wabawgamagau: Tomahawk; 1866 t.s. Ojibway notable.

Wabeneme: White Thunder; 1837 t.s. Ojibway notable.

Wabigoon: Marigold, or White Feather; First Nation of Ontario

Wabishkindib (ntg): Henry Conner; 1837 t.s. Ojibway notable.

Wabojeeg: White Fisher; 1837, 1854, 1863 t.s. Ojibway notable.

Wabokieshek: White Sky Light, or White Cloud, or The Light; aka The Winnebago Prophet; 1794-1841. Winnebago notable.

Wabonequaosh: White Hair; 1864 t.s. Ojibway notable.

Wadena: Little Round Hill. MN p.n.

Wageezhegome: Who Is Like the Day: aka Ogimauh binaessih: Chief Little Bird; aka John Cameron; Mississagua 1764-1828. Ojibway notable.

Wahdobekaung: Forest of Alders; Etobicoke; or Place Where Alders Grow. ON p.n.

Wahgoshig: Little Fox; First Nation of Ontario

Wahnapitae: Place Where Water is Shaped Like a Tooth; First Nation of Ontario

Wahta Mohawks: Sugar Maple; First Nation of Ontario

Waibejewung: Place Where the Waters Flow Back and Forth; aka Little Current; ON p.n.

Waishkey: Buffalo (U.P. river). MI p.n.

Waiter: Oscawbaywis; 1854 t.s. Ojibway notable.

Wakanjakoga: Coming Thunder: aka Winneshiek (the Younger); 1812-1872. Winnebago notable.

Wakaunhakah: Snake Skin; 1837 t.s. Winnebago notable.

Wakaunhononickah: Little Snake; 1832, 1837 t.s. Winnebago notable.

Wakaunkah (or Waukaunkaw): Snake; 1828, 1832, 1837 t.s. Winnebago notable.

Wakowush: Whippoorwill. (one Canadian treaty [CDN 124], signed in 1871, listed the signers as "Ojibway/Cree").

Wakunchakookah (various spellings): Yellow Thunder; 1837 t.s. 1774-1874. Winnebago notable.

Wakunchanickah: Little Thunder; 1837 t.s. Winnebago notable.

Wakuntchapinka: Good Thunder; c1790-1863. Winnebago notable.

Wakusheg: Foxes; source of Waukesha. WI p.n.

Walhahleigh: Watchful; aka Solomon George; 19th c. Oneida notable.

Walking To And Fro: Tedawkawmosay; 1863 t.s. Ojibway notable.

Walking Turtle: Karamanu; aka Nawkaw (ntg); 1735-1833. Winnebago notable.

Walking Turtle: Karraymaunee; aka Tshuonuzheekau: He Who Stands in the House; 1829, 1832 t.s. Winnebago notable.

Walking Turtle: Kayraymaunee; 1829 t.s. Winnebago notable.

Walks Naked: Khayratshoansaipkaw; 1832 t.s. Winnebago notable.

Walpole Island (Unceded Indian Territory); orig. Nissodjiwunaung: Three Channels; aka Bkejwanong Territory; Where the Waters Divide; Ontario First Nation.

Wametegoshins: Little Frenchman; 1837 t.s. Ojibway notable.

Wampum: Waymeekseegoo; 1828 t.s. Winnebago notable.

Wancahaga: Snake's Skin; 1825 t.s. Winnebago notable.

Wanig Suchka: Red Bird; 1788-1828. Winnebago notable.

Wanikamiu: Farthest Point of the Lake, or Fond du Lac: End of the Lake; French adaptation. Minnesota reservation.

Wanonchequa: Merchant; 1825 t.s. Winnebago notable.

Wanoshkang Bay: You Must Go Around; akaThomas Bay (on Manitoulin Island). ON p.n.

Wants Feathers: Iingegaunabe; 1864 t.s. Ojibway notable.

Wapachek: White Fisher; 1814 t.s. Ottawa notable.

Wapekeka: (ntg) (formerly known as Angling Lake First Nation); First Nation of Ontario

Wapmeme: White Pigeon; 1808 t.s. Ojibway notable.

War Chief: Wonaxilayhunka; aka Henry Roe Cloud; teacher, minister, educator; 1884-1950. Winnebago notable.

War Eagle: Horahoankkaw; 1832 t.s. Winnebago notable.

Warrior Prairie: Tuscola, or Level Lands. MI p.n.

Wasauksing: Place that Shines Brightly in the Reflection of the Sacred Light; formerly Parry Island First Nation of Ontario

Waseca: Rich, or Fertile (soil) . MN p.n.

Washagamis Bay: (also Obashkaandagaang) (ntg); First Nation of Ontario

Washaskkokone: Rat's Liver; 1837 t.s. Ojibway notable.

Washtenaw: On the River, or Far Off. MI p.n.

Wasp: Awmose; 1854 t.s. Ojibway notable.

Wassachum: First to Start the Whites; 1815 t.s. Ottawa notable.

Wasso: Bright Light, or Light Falling on a Distant Object; 1837 t.s. Ojibway notable.

Wastheelgo: Throwing Up Pins; aka Henry Powless; 19th c. Oneida notable.

Watashnewa: Bear's Legs; 1814 t.s. Ottawa notable.

Watchattykan: Big Boat; 1837 t.s. Winnebago notable.

Watchhatakaw: Big Canoe; 1855 t.s. Winnebago notable.

Watchkatoque: Grand Canoe; 1825 t.s. Winnebago notable.

Water (etc.): Kalamazoo, of Native origin, with several possible translations: It Smokes, Smoke, or Otter's Water; or from Kekekalakalamazoo: Where the Water Boils (or Smokes) in the Pot; or from Negikanamazo: Otter Tail, Beautiful Water, Boiling Water, or Stones Like Otters; or from Kikalamozo: He Is Inconvienced By Smoke In His Lodge. MI p.n.

Water (of the River) Is Clear: Wayaconuttaquayaw Sebe; original name for Eau Claire: French for Clear Water; WI p.n.

Water (or Waterfall) City: Minneapolis: from the Sioux 'Minne' plus the Greek 'apolis' (city). MN p.n.

Water of Light: Iosco. or Shining Water. MI p.n.

Water Reflecting Cloudy Skies; Minnesota, with several other translations: Cloudy, Sky colored, Whitish, or Milky Water; Reflection of Sky on Water; or Land of Many Lakes.

Waters Disappearing Underground, or Rumbling Waters: Shabwawagoning; possible source of Sheboygan: Needle, Awl, Disappearing River, Noise Underground, Reed Like, Thundering Under the Ground, or Something that Pierces. WI p.n. Michigan place name spelled Cheboygan.

Watonwan: Fish Bait Place, or Where Fish Abound. MN p.n.

Waudekaw: Little Hill; 1855 t.s. Ojibway notable.

Waukaumkaw: Rattle Snake; 1829 t.s. Winnebago notable.

Waukaunhahkaw: Snake Skin; 1828, 1829, 1832 t.s. Winnebago notable.

Waukaunkaw, or Wakaunkah: Snake; 1828, 1832, 1837 t.s. Winnebago notable.

Waukauntshaneekau: Deaf Thunder; 1829 t.s. Winnebago notable.

Waukauntshawhayreekaw: Roaring Thunder; 1832 t.s. Winnebago notable.

Waukauntshawwaykeewenkaw: Whirling Thunder; 1829, 1832 t.s. Winnebago notable.

Waukegan: Sheltering Place, or Trading Post. IL p.n.

Waukesha: from Wakusheg: Foxes. WI p.n.

Waukonhawkaw: White Eagle; aka Waukon Decora; ?-c1859. Winnebago notable.

Wauneehononik: Little Walker; 1832 t.s. Winnebago notable.

Waunkauntshawzeekau: Yellow Thunder; 1774-1874; 1829 t.s. Winnebago notable.

Waupaca: Clear Water Place. WI p.n.

Wausau: Far Away. WI p.n.

Wausaukee: Far Away Land. WI p.n.

Waushara: Good Land River, Big Fox, or Foxes. WI p.n.

Waussaukissing: Brightly Reflecting; original name for Parry Island; orig. ON p.n.

Wautsherookunahkaw: He Who Is Master of the Lodge; 1828, 1829 t.s. Winnebago notable.

Wauwi-autinoong: Round Lake. Original name for Lake St. Clair. MI, ON p.n.

Wawa: Cry of the Wild Goose, or simply Wild Goose. ON p.n.

Wawanosh: Beautiful Sailor. ON p.n.

Wawbawnemeke: White Thunder; 1854 t.s. Ojibway notable.

Wawhecoochawhoonokaw: Little Thunder; 1855 t.s. Winnebago notable.

Wawiyatanong (Where the River Turns, or Crooked Way), original name for Detroit. Also, Yondotiga: Great Village; or Karontaen: Coast of the Straits. MI p.n.

Wawkonchawkoohaw: Coming Thunder; aka Winnoshik (ntg); 1855 t.s. Winnebago notable.

Wawsaygezhick: Clear Sky; 1854 t.s. Ojibway notable.

Wayaconuttaquayaw Sebe: Water (of the River) Is Clear; aka Eau Claire: French for Clear Water. WI p.n.

Waymeekseegoo: Wampum; 1828 t.s. Winnebago notable.

Waysawagwonaib: Yellow Feather; 1863 t.s. Ojibway notable.

Wazaukonia: Yellow Robe; 1837 t.s. Ojibway notable.

Weabskewen: White Man; 1817 t.s. Ojibway notable.

Webster, Thomas; aka Hayahdugihwah: Bitter Body; Onondaga; 19th c. keeper of the wampum for the League of the Iroquois. Iroquois notable.

Weescoup: Sucre; 1825 t.s. Ojibway notable.

Weeskonsan: Gathering of the Waters; possible source of Wisconsin: possible meanings: Muskrat Land, Grassy Place; or from Meskousing: Where the Waters Gather, Place of the Red Earth People, or Red Stone; or from Misconsin: Strong Current.

Weetshahunkuk: Forked Tail; 1832 t.s. Winnebago notable.

Weetshunkaw: Goose; 1832 t.s. Winnebago notable.

Welling Waters Place: Batchewana Bay. ON p.n.

Wenghegesheguk: First Day; 1837 t.s. Ojibway notable.

West Bay (Manitoulin Is); orig. Mitchigee-waedinong: Bare West Place. Ontario First Nation.

Wet Mouth: Kabemabe; 1837 t.s. Ojibway notable.

Weweshanshis: Bad Boy; aka Big Mouth; 1837 t.s. Ojibway notable.

Weyauwega: Here We Rest. WI p.n.

Wheankkaw: Duck; 1828 t.s. Winnebago notable.

Wheeling Creek: from Wihling: Place of the Head. PA p.n.

Where Fish Abound: Watonwan; or Fish Bait Place. MN p.n.

Where It Is Noisy, or Smoke (in reference to mist from falls): Quinnesec Falls. WI p.n.

Where River and Lake Meet: Cataraqui. ON p.n.

Where the Current Begins, River Flowing Into the Lake, or River Flowing Into Another Body of Water: Mattawa. ON p.n.

Where the River Turns (or Crooked Way), from Wawiyatanong. Original name for Detroit. Also, Yondotiga: Great Village; or Karontaen: Coast of the Straits. MI p.n.

Where the Rocks Strike Together: Neechahkekoonahonah; original name for Wisconsin Dells. WI p.n.

Where the Sand Slides Down the Bank, or Place of White Falling Sands: Penetanguishene. ON p.n.

Where the Water is Shallow: Baagwaashiing; new name for Pays Plat (French: Flat Land) First Nation of Ontario

Where the Waters Gather, Place of the Red Earth People, or Red Stone: Meskousing; possible source of Wisconsin: with possible meanings: Muskrat Land, Grassy Place; or from Misconsin: Strong Current; or from Weeskonsan: Gathering of the Waters.

Where There Are Forks: Lechauweeki; source of Lehigh; or from Lechauwekink: At the Falls. PA p.n.

Where There Is a Fort: Menachksink; original name for Pittsburgh. PA p.n.

Where They Take the Boats Out: Cayuga; from Gaw Ugwck: IN p.n. Ontario Tribe/First Nation.

Whippoorwill: Wakowush; (one Canadian treaty [CDN 124], signed in 1871, listed the signers as "Ojibway/Cree").

Whirling Thunder: Waukauntshawwaykeewenkaw; 1829, 1832 t.s. Winnebago notable.

Whirlpool: Neehookaw; 1828 t.s. Winnebago notable.

White Bear: Hoantshskawskaw; 1832 t.s. Winnebago notable.

White Breast: Maunkshawka; 1829 t.s. Winnebago notable.

White Clay Place: Gawababigunikag Sagaiigun: the White Earth Reservation; aka Gawababiganikag: White Clay. MN p.n.

White Cloud, The Light, or White Sky Light: Wabokieshek; aka The Winnebago Prophet; 1794-1841. Winnebago notable.

White Cloud: Wabanaquot; 1830-1898. Ojibway notable.

White Crow: Kaureekausawkaw; 1828, 1832 t.s. Winnebago notable.

White Crow: Pishkagaghe; 1837 t.s. Ojibway notable.

White Dog: Shaonkskawkaw; 1828 t.s. Winnebago notable.

White Eagle: Waukonhawkaw; aka Waukon Decora; ?-c1859. Winnebago notable.

White Earth Reservation; aka Gawababiganikag: White Clay, or Gawababigunikag Sagaiigun: White Clay Place. MN p.n.

White Elk: Hoowayskaw; 1832 t.s. Winnebago notable.

White Feather or Marigold: Wabigoon First Nation (Ontario)

White Fisher: Wabojeeg; 1837, 1854, 1863 t.s. Ojibway notable.

White Fisher: Wapachek; 1814 t.s. Ottawa notable.

White Hair: Wabonequaosh; 1864 t.s. Ojibway notable.

White Head: Theyanoguin; aka King Hendrick; aka Hendrick Peters; sachem, diplomat; c1680-1755. Mohawk notable.

White Man: Weabskewen; 1817 t.s. Ojibway notable.

White Ox: Cheyskawkaw; 1829 t.s. Winnebago notable.

White Pigeon: Wapmeme; 1808 t.s. Ojibway notable.

White Potato: Macoupin. IL p.n.

White Thunder: Wabeneme; 1837 t.s. Ojibway notable.

White Thunder: Wawbawnemeke; 1854 t.s. Ojibway notable.

White War Eagle: Heetshawausharpskawkau; 1829, 1832 t.s. Winnebago notable.

White Water: Wabash, or Bog River, or Pure White (in reference to its limestone bed). IL, IN p.n.

White, Angus; aka Enneasnekauntaa: Small Stick of Wood; 19th c. Snipe clan leader. Mohawk notable.

White, Charles; aka Sarothanewana: Two Hide Together; 19th c. Wolf clan leader. Mohawk notable.

White: Ohio. PA p.n.

Whitefish Lake: former name for Atikameksheng Anishnawbek First Nation (of Ontario)

Whitefish Point People: Naotkamegwanning Anishinabe First Nation (Ontario)

Whitesand: First Nation of Ontario

Whitewater Lake: First Nation of Ontario

Whitish, or Milky Water; Minnesota, with several other translations: Cloudy, Sky colored, Water Reflecting Cloudy Skies; Reflection of Sky on Water; or Land of Many Lakes.

Who Is Like the Day: Wageezhegome; aka Ogimauh-binaessih: Chief Little Bird; aka John Cameron; Mississagua 1764-1828. Ojibway notable.

Who Puts Things in Order: Tekakwitha (Kateri): or She Hesitates; aka The Lily of the Mohawks; Mohawk spiritual woman made a Saint by the Roman Catholic church in 2012; 1656-1680. IL p.n.

Wickedly Expert: Acqueweezais, or Expert Boy. 1837 t.s. Ojibway notable.

Wihling: Place of the Head; source of Wheeling Creek. PA p.n.

Wikwemikong (Manitoulin Is.): Beaver Bay; Unceded Indian Territory. Ontario First Nation.

Wild Cat: Heetshaumwaukaw; 1829 t.s. Winnebago notable.

Wild Cat: Thaunwankaw; 1828 t.s. Winnebago notable.

Wild Duck, or To Cross a Point, or Prairie Hen: Kewaunee: from Kakiweonan: Land Crossing By Boat. WI p.n.

Wild Goose, or Cry of the Wild Goose: Wawa. ON p.n.

Wild Goose, or Snapping Turtle: Peshtigo. WI p.n.

Wild Pigeon Place: Mimico. ON p.n.

Wild Rice People: Menominee: Men of the Good Seed; Wisconsin tribe. MI p.n.

Wild Rice: Mahnomen. MN p.n.

Williams, Eleazar; aka Onwarenhiiaki: Tree Cutter; claimed to be the Lost Dauphin of France; controversial preacher; 1788-1858. Mohawk notable.

Williams, Thomas: akaTehoragwanegen: He Has Placed Two Worlds Together; c1758-1849. Mohawk notable.

Wind: Naudin; 1825, 1837 t.s. Ojibway notable.

Wing of the Wild Swan Dyed Scarlet: Red Wing: from Koopoohoosha. MN p.n.

Winisk, now called Peawanuck: Flintstone. ON p.n.

Winnebago Prophet (The); aka Wabokieshek: White Cloud, The Light, or White Sky Light; 1794-1841. Winnebago notable.

Winnebago: said to be from a Potawatomi word, Winpyeko, which means People of the Dirty Water, in reference to Green Bay, Wisconsin, their traditional homeland; also said to mean Fish Eaters, or People of the Sea; self designations are Hochunkgra: People of the Big

Voice, Hutcangara: Big Fish People, or Hochagra: People of the Parent Speech; the Wisconsin tribe has officially changed its name to Ho-chunk Nation: People of the First Voice; Nebraska, Minnesota, Wisconsin tribe; IL, MN, NE, WI p.n.

Winner: Kehbehnawgay; 1863 t.s. Ojibway notable.

Winneshiek (the Younger); aka Wakanjakoga: Coming Thunder; 1812-1872. Winnebago notable.

Winnoshik (ntg); aka Coming Thunder: Wawkonchawkoohaw; 1855 t.s. Winnebago notable.

Winona: First Born (if a daughter). IN, MI, MN p.n.

Winpyeko: People of the Dirty Water, in reference to Green Bay, Wisconsin, their traditional homeland; aka the Winnebago; might also mean Fish Eaters, or People of the Sea; self designations said to be Hochunkgra: People of the Big Voice, Hutcangara: Big Fish People, or Hochagra: People of the Parent Speech; the Wisconsin tribe has officially changed its name to Ho-chunk Nation: People of the First Voice; Nebraska, Wisconsin tribe; IL, MN, NE, WI p.n.

WISCONSIN: possible meanings: Muskrat Land, Grassy Place; or from Meskousing: Where the Waters Gather, Place of the Red Earth People, or Red Stone; or from Misconsin: Strong Current; or from Weeskonsan: Gathering of the Waters.

Wisconsin Dells; orig. Neechahkekoonahonah: Where the Rocks Strike Together. WI p.n.

Wisconsin tribe: Munsee People of the Stoney Country; aka Muncie; Lenni Lenape sub tribe; The Stockbridge Munsee are an amalgamated tribe of Stockbridge people made up of Mahican, and other Algonkians, and the Munsee. Moved by the government to Wisconsin from the northeast in the 1840s.

Wisconsin Tribe; the Oneida; from Onuyo'teaka': People of the Standing (or Upright) Stone, or Stone People; or from Onayotekäono: Granite People; aka Ratirontakowa: People of the Big Log; New York, Ontario, Wisconsin tribe; part of the Iroquois Conf.; NY, TN, WI p.n.

Without Horns: Hayrokawkaw; 1828 t.s. Winnebago notable.

Woanknawhoapeenekaw: Big Medicine Man; 1829 t.s. Winnebago notable.

Woankshikrootshkay: Man Eater; 1829 t.s. Winnebago notable.

Wolf Land: Kankakee. IL p.n.

Wolf: Mahican; or from Muh-heconneok: People of the Waters that Are Never Still (a reference to the Hudson River). WI tribe.

Wolf's Mountain Home Maker: Kehachiwinga; aka Haksigaxunuminka: Little Fish Daughter; aka Mountain Wolf Woman; writer; 1884-1960. Winnebago notable.

Woman Coming on the Clouds in Glory, or Fleecy Cloud Floating Into Place: Hinookmahiwi-Kilinaka; aka Angel DeCora Dietz; artist, writer, activist; c1871-1919. Winnebago notable.

Wonaxilayhunka; War Chief; aka Henry Roe Cloud; teacher, minister, educator; 1884-1950. Winnebago notable.

Wood, Joseph; aka Sosesaisnesakeken: Snow Crust; 19th c. Heron clan leader. Mohawk notable.

Wood: Nankaw; 1828 t.s. Winnebago notable.

Wood: Naukawkarymaunie; 1829 t.s. Winnebago notable.

Wood's Spirit: Manistee (and Manistique); or Crooked River, or Red River, or Wind Sound, or Lost River. MI p.n.

Woodpecker: Paquaamo; 1837 t.s. Ojibway notable.

Wunnumin: Lake of Beaver Meal Fragments; or from Onumananing: Red Paint, or Vermillion. Ontario First Nation.

Wyandotte: Islanders, or Peninsula Dwellers. MI, OH p.n.

Wyoming: from M'chevomi: Extensive Flats. PA p.n.

- *y* -

Yabanse: Young Buck; 1837 t.s. Ojibway notable.

Yellow Bank: Hazeekaw; 1855 t.s. Winnebago notable.

Yellow Earth People: Osaukie-uck: source of Sauk. IL, WI p.n.

Yellow Earth Place, or Mouth of the River: Ozaukee. WI p.n.

Yellow Feather: Waysawagwonaib; 1863 t.s. Ojibway notable.

Yellow Head: Musquakie; 1868 t.s. (CDN 18). Ojibway notable.

Yellow Medicine: from; Pezhihutazizi Kapi: Diggings of Yellow Plant Root (Moonseed). MN p.n.

Yellow Paint: Salamonie:. IN p.n.

Yellow Quill: Oozawekwun; (one Canadian treaty [CDN 124], signed in 1871, listed the signers as "Ojibway/Cree").

Yellow River: from Waythowkahmik: Yellow Waters. IN p.n.

Yellow Robe: Wazaukonia; 1837 t.s. Ojibway notable.

Yellow Thunder: Wakunchakukah or Wakunchakookah; 1837 t.s.; 1774-1874. Winnebago notable.

Yellow Track, He that Leaves the: Sawwaughkeewau; 1828 t.s. Winnebago notable.

Yellow Waters: from Waythowkahmik: Yellow Waters. IN p.n.

Yellow: Necedah. WI p.n.

Yellowhead, William: aka Musquakie; d.1864 (possible father to next). Ojibway notable.

Yenrash: It Is Long-tailed, or Panther; possible source of Erie: Cougar (or Panther) Place. PA p.n.

Yondotiga: Great Village. Original name for Detroit. Also, Wawiyatanong: Where the River Turns, or Crooked Way; or Karontaen: Coast of the Straits. MI p.n.

Yorke, Johnathan: aka Mesquab (ntg); artist; fl. 1900s. Ojibway notable.

You Must Go Around: Wanoshkang Bay; aka Thomas Bay (on Manitoulin Island). ON p.n.

Young Boy: Oscaquassanu; 1805 t.s. Ojibway notable.

Young Buck: Yabanse; 1837 t.s. Ojibway notable.

Young Buffalo: Pezhekins; 1837 t.s. Ojibway notable.

Young Chief: Okemance; 1817 t.s. (see Ogimaus, above). Ojibway notable.

Young Man's Son: Nawboneaush, or Naybunacaush; 1855, 1863 t.s. Ojibway notable.

Young Ox: Peshawkay; 1795 t.s. Ojibway notable.

Youth: Oskenawway; 1854 t.s. Ojibway notable.

Yuma: Sons of the River. MI p.n.

- Z -

Zaagiing: At the Mouth of the River; source of Saugeen First Nation (Ontario).

Zeba: from Zibii: River. MI Place name.

Zheewegonab: Duck Feather; fl. 1780-1805. Ojibway notable.

Zhiibaahaasing: (ntg) (formerly Cockburn Island 19A); First Nation of Ontario

Zhuawuno-geezhigo-gaubow: He Who Stands in the Southern Sky; aka Maisaninnine: Stylish Person; aka Jack Fiddler; c1830-1907. Ojibway notable.

U.S. Treaties

Map Number	Year Signed	Location of signing	Tribe or Tribes
001-PA	1784	Fort Stanwix (NY)	Six Nations of New York.
011-IN-OH	1795	Greenville (OH)	Wyandot, Delaware, Ottawa, Chippewa, Potawatomi, Miami, Eel River, Wea, Kickapoo, Piankishaw, Kaskaskia.
025-IN	Same as 011.		
026-IN	Same as 011.		
048-IL	1803	Vincennes (IN)	Kaskaskia.
049-IN	1804	Vincennes (IN)	Delaware.
050-IL	1804	St. Louis (MO)	Sauk and Fox.
053-OH –	1805	Fort Industry, on the Miami of the Lake	Wyandot, Ottawa, Chippewa, Munsee, Delaware, Shawnee, Potawatomi
054-OH	Same as 053.		
056-IN	1805	Grouseland, near Vincennes (IN)	Delaware, Potawatomi, Miami, Eel River, Wea.
063-IL	1805	Vincennes (IN)	Piankishaw.
066-MI-OH	1807	Detroit	Ottawa, Chippewa, Wyandot, Potawatomi.
071-IN	1809	Fort Wayne (IN)	Delaware, Potawatomi, Miami, Eel River Miami.
072-IN	Same as 071.		
073-IL-IN	1809	Vincennes	Kickapoo.
078-IL	1816	St. Louis	Ottawa, Chippewa, Potawatomi.
087-OH-MI	1817	Foot of the rapids of the Miami of Lake Erie	Wyandot, Seneka, Delaware, Shawnee, Potawatomi, Ottawa, Chippewa.
088-OH	Same as 087.		

096a-IL	1818	Edwardsville (IL)	Peoria, Kaskaskia, Mitchigamia, Cahokia, Tamaroa.
098-IL-IN	1818	St. Mary's (OH)	Potawatomi.
099-IN-OH	1818	St. Mary's (OH)	Miami.
111-MI	1819	Saginaw, Michigan Territory	Chippewa.
117-IN-MI	1821	Chicago	Ottawa, Chippewa, Potawatomi.
132-IN	1826	Near the mouth of Mississippi River, on the Wabash	Potawatomi.
133-IN	Same as 132.		
142-IN	1828	Wyandot village near the Wabash in Indiana	Eel river or Thorntown party of Miami Indians
145-MI	1828	St. Joseph missionary establishment (MI)	Potawatomi.
146-IN	Same as 145.		
177-IL	1832	Camp Tippecanoe (IN)	Potawatomi (band of the Prairie and Kanakakee).
180-IN	1832	Tippacanoe River (IN)	Potawatomi.
181-IN	Same as 180		
190-MI	1833	Chicago	Chippewa, Ottawa, Potawatomi.
198-IN	1834	Forks of the Wabash in Indiana	Miami.
205-MI	1836	Washington, DC	Ottawa and Chippewa.
242-MN-WI	1837	St. Peter's River where it meets the Mississippi (WI)	Chippewa.
243-MN	1837	Washington, DC	Sioux.
258-IN	1840	Forks of the Wabash (IN)	Miami.
261-MI-WI	1842	La Pointe of Lake Superior (WI)	Chippewa of the Mississippi and Lake Superior.
268-MN	1847	Fond Du Lac of Lake Superior	Chippewa of the Mississippi and Lake Superior.
269-MN	1847	Leech Lake	Chippewa (Pillager band).

289-MN	1851	Traverse des Sioux (MN)	Sioux (Sisseton and Wahpeton bands).
332-MN	1854	La Pointe (WI)	Chippewa of Lake Superior and the Mississippi.
357-MN	1855	Washington, DC	Chippewa of the Mississippi.
413-MN	1858	Washington, DC	Sioux (Medewakanton and Wahpeton bands).
440-MN/1863	Act of Congress	Chippewa of Mississippi, and Pillager and Lake Winnibigoshish bands of Chippewa.	
445-MN	1863	Old crossing of Red Lake River (MN)	Chippewa (Red Lake and Pembina bands)
446-MN	Same as 445.		
457-MN	1864	Washington, DC	Chippewa of Mississippi, and Pillager and Lake Winnibigoshish bands of Chippewa.
482-MN	1866	Washington, DC	Chippewa (Bois Fort band).
483-MN	Same as 482.		
706-MN North	1889	Agreement	Chippewa of Minnesota,
707-MN North	1889	Agreement	Red Lake Chippewa.
708-MN North	1889	Agreement	Pembina Chippewa.
709-MN North	1889	Agreement	Minnesota Chippewa of White Earth Reservation.
710-MN North	1889	Agreement	White Oak Band of Mississippi Chippewa, Pillager and Winnibigoshish bands.

Canadian Treaties

Ontario Treaties Designated By Letter Code On Maps

Letter Code	Date Signed	Treaty Name	Tribe or Tribes
A	1783	Crawfords Treaty	Mississauga.
AA	1854	Treaty 72	Chippewa.
AB	1857	Treaty 82	Chippewa.
AC	1873	Treaty 3	Ojibway.
AD	1873	Treaty 5	Saulteaux and Swampy Cree.
AE	1905, 1906	James Bay Treaty 9	Ojibway and Cree.
AF	1923	Williams Treaty	Chippewa.
AG	1923	Williams Treaty	Chippewa.
AH	1929	Adhesion to Treaty 9.	
B	1783	Crawfords Treaty	Algonquin and Iroquois.
C	1790	Treaty 2	Ottawa, Chippewa, Potawatomi, Huron.
D	1792	Treaty 3	Mississagua.
E	1781	Treaty 381	Mississagua and Chippewa.
F	1793	Tyendinaga Twp. To Mohawks.	
G	1795	Treaty 3-3/4	Mississauga.
H	1795	Treaty 5	Chippewa.
I	1796	Treaty 6	Chippewa.
J	1796	Treaty 7	Chippewa.
K	1798	Treaty 11	Chippewa.
L	1805	Treaty 13	Mississauga.
M	1805	Treaty 13a	Mississauga.
N	1815	Treaty 16	Chippewa.

O	1818	Treaty 18	Chippewa.
P	1918	Treaty 19	Mississauga.
Q	1818	Treaty 20	Chippewa.
R	1819	Treaty 21	Chippewa.
S	1819	Treaty 27	Mississauga.
T	1925	Treaty 27-1/2	Ojibway and Chippewa.
U	1833	Treaty 35	Wyandot or Huron.
V	1836	Treaty 45	Chippewa and Ottawa.
W	1836	Treaty 45-1/2	Saugeen.
X	1847	Treaty 57	Iroquois of St. Regis.
Y	1850	Robinson-Superior Treaty 60.	Ojibway
Z	1850	Robinson-Huron Treaty 61	Ojibway.

References

Abate, Frank R., ed. <u>American Places Dictionary</u>. Detroit: Omnigraphics Inc., 1994.

Baker, Ronald L. & Marvin Carmony. <u>Indiana Place Names</u>. Bloomington: IN U P, 1975.

Baroy, Brant. Mohawks of the Bay of Quinte, Ont.

Bellfy, Phil. <u>Indians and Other Misnomers: A Cross-Reference Dictionary of the People, Persons, and Places of Native North America</u>. Golden, Colo.: Fulcrum Pub., 2001. Benson, Sandy. St. Croix Council, WI.

Canada. <u>Indian Treaties & Surrenders</u>. Toronto/Ottawa: Canadiana House 1973. 3 vols.

Champagne, Duane, ed. <u>Native North America Almanac</u>. Detroit: Gale Research, 1994.

Clifton, James A. <u>The Prairie People: Continuity & Change in Potawatomi Indian Culture, 1665-1965</u>. Lawrence: Regents P of Kansas, c1977.

Commanda, Karen. Nipissing Indian Band, Ont.

Davis, Mary B., ed. <u>Native America in the Twentieth Century</u>. NY: Garland Pub., 1994).

<u>Dictionary of Canadian Biography</u>. Toronto: U of Toronto P, 1966- 13 vols.

Dockstader, Frederick J. <u>Great North American Indians</u>. NY: Van Nostrand Reinhold, c1977.

Donehoo, George P. <u>A History of the Indian Village Place Names in Pennsylvania</u>. Baltimore: Gateway P Inc., 1977 (reprint of 1928, Harrisburg: Telegraph P, edition).

Upham, Warren. <u>Minnesota Geographic Names: Their Origin & Historical Significance</u>. St. Paul: Minn. Hist. Soc, 1969 (reprint edition).

Gard, Robert Edward. <u>The Romance of Wisconsin Place Names</u>. NY: October House Inc., 1968.

Garland, G.D. <u>Names of Algonquin: Stories Behind the Lake and Place Names of Algonquin Provincial Park</u>. Algonquin Park Tech. Bull. No. 10, 1991.

Canadian Geographical Names Database. https://www.nrcan.gc.ca/earth-sciences/geography/querying-canadian-geographical-names-database/canadian-geographical-names-database/19870

Grand Traverse Band of Ottawa, MI.

Hamilton, William B. <u>The Macmillan Book of Canadian Place Names</u>. Toronto: Macmillan, 1978.

Hodge, Frederick Webb. <u>Handbook of American Indians North of Mexico</u>. Wash. DC: GPO, 1912 (two vols.).

Holmer, Nils M. <u>Indian Place Names in North America</u>. Cambridge: Harvard UP, 1948.

Johnston, Basil H. <u>By Canoe & Moccasin: Some Native Place Names of the Great Lakes</u>. Lakefield, Ont.: Waapoone Pub. & Promotion, 1986.

Kappler, Charles J. <u>Indian Treaties, 1778-1883</u>. NY: Interland Pub., 1972.

Kelton, Dwight H. <u>Indian Names of Places Near the Great Lakes</u>. Detroit: Detroit Free Press Printing, 1888.

LeBlanc, Kathy. Bay Mills Indian Community, MI.

Leitch, Barbara A. <u>A Concise Dictionary of Indian Tribes of North America</u>. Algonac, MI: Reference Pub. Inc., 1979.

Lindsey, David. <u>Ohio's Western First Nation: The Story of its Place Names</u>. Cleveland: P of Western First Nation U, 1955.

Malinowski, Sharon, ed. <u>Notable Native Americans</u>. Detroit: Gale Research, 1995.

McGranahan, Jill. The power of place names. https://red.msudenver.edu/2022/the-power-of-place-names/

Miami Nation of Indiana.

Moore, W.F. <u>Indian Place Names in Ontario</u>. Toronto: Macmillan, 1930.

Myers, Charlie. Northern Michigan Ottawa.

Rayburn, Alan. <u>Naming Canada: Stories About Place Names from Canadian Geographic</u>. Toronto: U of Toronto P, 1994.

Reichel, Wm. C. <u>Names Which the Lenni Lenape or Delaware Indians Gave to Rivers, Streams, and Localities Within the States of Pennsylvania, New Jersey, Maryland, and Virginia</u>. 1872 PAH-I-1407).

Royce, Charles C.; William, Nelson Edward; Powell, John Wesley, and Smithsonian Institution. 1899. <u>Eighteenth Annual Report of the Bureau of American Ethnology to the Secretary of the Smithsonian Institution 1896-97</u>. Washington D.C: G.P.O.

Scott, David E. <u>Ontario Place Names</u>. Vancouver: Whitecap Books, 1993.

Scugog Indian Band, Ont.

Shearer, Benjamin F. & Barbara S. Shearer. <u>State Names, Seals, Flags, & Symbols</u>. Westport, CT: Greenwood P, 1994.

Stockbridge-Munsee Tribal Council, WI.

Tiller, Veronica E. Velarde, ed. <u>Federal & State Indian Reservations & Trust Areas</u>. U.S. Dept. of Commerce, 1996.

Tyrrell, J.B. <u>Algonquin Indian Names of Places in Northern Canada</u>. Toronto: Canada House, 1968 (reprint of 1915 ed.).

U.S. Board on Geographic Names. https://www.usgs.gov/us-board-on-geographic-names/domestic-names

Vogel, Virgil. <u>Indian Names on Wisconsin's Map</u>. NP: U of WI P, 1991.

Waldman, Carl. <u>Encyclopedia of Native American Tribes</u>. NY: Facts on File, 1988.

Waldman, Carl. <u>Atlas of the North American Indian</u>. NY: Facts of File, 1985.

Waldman, Carl. <u>Who Was Who in Native American History</u>. NY: Facts on File, 1990.

Wolk, Allen. <u>The Naming of America</u>. NY: Cornerstone Lib., 1977.

About the Author

Phil Bellfy is an enrolled member of the White Earth Band of Minnesota Chippewa, and Professor Emeritus of American Indian Studies, Michigan State University. He resides in Michigan's Eastern Upper Peninsula near Sault Ste. Marie. Dr. Bellfy is also the Founder and a Co-Director of Center for the Study of Indigenous Border Issues (CSIBI) and serves as the Editor and Publisher of its education imprint, the Ziibi Press (see below).

BOOKS BY PHIL BELLFY
Authored:

UP Colony: A Brief History of Resource Exploitation in Michigan's Upper Peninsula, with a Focus on Sault Manufacturing. Ziibi Press, 2021. Winner of 2021 U.P. Notable Books Award,

Three Fires Unity: The Anishnaabeg of the Lake Huron Borderlands. Winner of the University of Nebraska Press "North American Indian Prose Award" in 2011. . Winner of 2020 U.P. Notable Books Award.

Indians and Other Misnomers: a Cross-referenced Dictionary of the People, Persons, and Places of Native North America. Golden, CO: Fulcrum Press, 2001. A cross-referenced dictionary of tribal names, historical figures, and notable place names of North America, utilizing *traditional* names (with translation).

First Americans Engagement Calendar. (Co-author with Judith Dupré) NY: Random House, 1993, 1994, 1995. Dr. Bellfy researched and wrote a historical notation about a significant event in Native American History for each day of the calendar year. New material was presented in each of the three editions. The 1993 edition received the *Bronze Award* for the "Best Theme - Desk Calendar" from the Calendar Marketing Association. The 1994 edition won the *Silver Award* in the same competition.

Edited:

Joe Pete. Written by Florence McClinchey; first published in 1929 by Henry Holt. 2018 Edition edited by Phil Bellfy; published by Ziibi Press. The novel is set on Sugar Island, near Sault Ste. Marie, and the main characters are Indigenous people who live on the island.

Big John. Written by Florence McClinchey; First published by Ziibi Press in 2018; edited by Phil Bellfy; The "long-lost" sequel to *Joe Pete*, the novel is also set on Sugar Island, situated near the US/Canada border near Sault Ste. Marie.

Honor the Earth: Great Lakes Indigenous Response to Environmental Crises. Edited by Phil Bellfy. Published by Ziibi Press, 2014, 2020 (2nd Edition).

So You Want To Go To Graduate School? By Kenneth L. Poff and William Gordon. Edited by Phil Bellfy. Published by Ziibi Press, 2010, Sault Ste. Marie, MI.

About Ziibi Press:

The Ziibi Press is the publishing arm of CSIBI, the Center for the Study of Indigenous Border Issues. "Ziibi" is the Ojibway word for "river," as in Mississippi (Ki-chi-ziibi; "a really big river"). CSIBI is focused on the political, economic, and cultural boundaries that separate Indigenous People from each other and the elements of the more dominant societies. It is with this focus that this volume covers the entire Upper Great Lakes, both US and Canada.

In the 1980s, Phil Bellfy pondered the question: Why does Sault, Ontario, appear to be so prosperous, while the "Sault" on the American side has fallen into such a deplorable state? Could the answer be that the "American side" was little more than a "resource colony"-or to use the academic jargon of "Conflict and Change" Sociology-an "Internal Colony." In UP Colony, Bellfy revisits his graduate research to update us the state of the Sault.

The ultimate question: why has the U.P.'s vast wealth, nearly unrivaled in the whole of the United States, left the area with poverty nearly unrivaled in the whole of the United States? None of the conventional explanations from "distance to markets," to "too many people," to "disadvantageous production costs," have any credibility. Simply put: "Where did the $1.5 billion earned from copper mining, $1 billion from logging, and nearly $4 billion in iron ore go?"

To get to the bottom of these thorny questions, Bellfy looks at the possible economic pressures imposed by "external colonial powers." The pressure-points examined in this book include presence of a complimentary economy, lopsided investment in one sector, monopoly style management, disparity of living standards, a repressive conflict-resolution system, and the progressive growth of inequality over time.

In *UP Colony*, Dr. Bellfy has revisited his MA Thesis and brought this analysis up-to-date in conjunction with the Sault's Semisepticentennial-the 350th anniversary of its French founding in 1668.

"There are many people who will benefit from reading this book: academic readers and researchers; nonfiction writers working on similar themes; and more "creative" authors who want to get the facts straight, whatever their projects. The extensive bibliography will be helpful to many of these readers, too. *UP Colony* is a fairly quick read and easy to follow with its typical academic format of stating a premise/theory, organizing the points of the argument, supporting that argument with facts and statistics, and finally drawing a conclusion."
-- Deborah K. Frontiera, *U.P. Book Review*

"Bellfy's deft rural sociological analysis cuts through centuries of whitewashing and exploitation with a single stroke."
-- Victor R. Volkman, *Marquette Monthly*

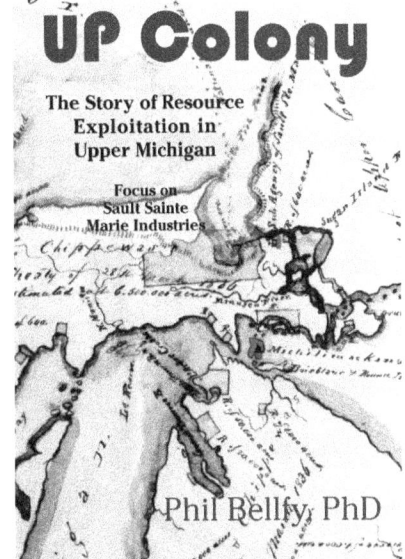

From Ziibi press
www.ZiibiPress.com

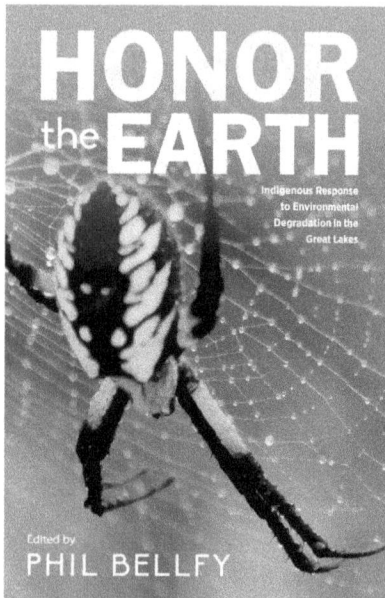

HONOR
the EARTH

Indigenous Response
to Environmental
Degradation in the
Great Lakes

Edited by
PHIL BELLFY

The Great Lakes Basin is under severe ecological threat from fracking, bursting pipelines, sulfide mining, abandonment of government environmental regulation, invasive species, warming and lowering of the lakes, etc. This book presents essays on Traditional Knowledge, Indigenous Responsibility, and how Indigenous people, governments, and NGOs are responding to the environmental degradation which threatens the Great Lakes. This volume grew out of a conference that was held on the campus of Michigan State University on Earth Day, 2007.

All of the essays have been updated and revised for this book. Among the presenters were Ward Churchill (author and activist), Joyce Tekahnawiiaks King (Director, Akwesasne Justice Department), Frank Ettawageshik, (Executive Director of the United Tribes of Michigan), Aaron Payment (Chair of the Sault Sainte Marie Tribe of Chippewa Indians), and Dean Sayers (Chief of the Batchewana First Nation). Winona LaDuke (author, activist, twice Green Party VP candidate) also contributed to this volume.

Adapted from the Introduction by Dr. Phil Bellfy:

The elements of the relationship that the Great Lakes' ancient peoples had with their environment, developed over the millennia, was based on respect for the natural landscape, pure and simple. The "original people" of this area not only maintained their lives, they thrived within the natural boundaries established by their relationship with the natural world. In today's vocabulary, it may be something as simple as an understanding that if human beings take care of the environment, the environment will take care of them. The entire relationship can be summarized as harmony and balance, based on respect.

"*Honor the Earth* is a deep dive into indigenous culture, beliefs, and their close relationship to nature and the environment. It is provocative, disturbing, and to the point. And the point is that humanity is 'killing the natural world, and thus itself.' It's no more complicated than that."
-- Tom Powers, *Michigan in Books*

"Let's not beat around the bush, we are in trouble! This book provides some very important perspectives from an Indigenous lens about the condition of the Mother Earth and our behaviors as humans." --Martin Reinhardt, Professor of Native American Studies at Northern Michigan University

From Ziibi Press

www.ZiibiPress.com

www.ingramcontent.com/pod-product-compliance
Lightning Source LLC
Chambersburg PA
CBHW080614270326
41928CB00016B/3063